SECRETS OF SELLING TO THE SUPER RICH

SECRETS OF SELLING TO THE SUPER RICH

SALES SUPERSTARS OF LUXURY

Doug Gollan, Michael Calman & Daniel Wade

HUDSON RIDGE BOOKS

2016

HUDSON RIDGE BOOKS

650 West 42nd Street, Suite 2212
New York, NY 10036

ISBN-13: 9781533467225
ISBN-10: 1533467226
Library of Congress Control Number: 2016908681
CreateSpace Independent Publishing Platform
North Charleston, South Carolina

CONTENTS

Praise for—
Secrets of Selling to the Super Rich

"I've had the good fortune to know Doug Gollan and Michael Calman, former SVP Marketing Bergdorf Goodman, for more than 20 years. Time after time I have consistently been the beneficiary of their incisive strategic marketing insights and counsel. Their new book (with third co-author—Daniel Wade) *Secrets of Selling to the Super Rich: Sales Superstars of Luxury* is a grand-slam home run, bases loaded, eleventh inning, knocked right out of the park, known as 'Strategic Insights & Best Practices You Can Use.' Eight compelling interviews with world class luminaries in beauty, fine jewelry, travel, publishing, private jets, tourism and hospitality offer a wealth of marketing insights that challenge luxury marketers to think more creatively and practically. Their work is a breakthrough breath of strategic fresh air that will inspire the most sophisticated, marketing-savvy brands to take a new look at what they do and how to do even better and more profitably."

Gregory J. Furman
Founder & Chairman
The Luxury Marketing Council (since 1994)
The Young Luxury Marketers' Council (since 2011)

"How do you utilize branding, marketing, social media, and most critically, the power of relationships, to sell to the Super Rich? This insider guide, informed by experts throughout the industry will show you how to become a trusted purveyor to this exclusive market."

Matthew D. Upchurch, CTC
Chairman & CEO, Virtuoso

PREFACE

C reating Secrets of Selling to the Super Rich was inspired by the pursuit of a better understanding about the distinctive attitudes, exclusive activities, and most particularly, the purchasing behaviors of Ultra High Net Worth (UHNW) individuals, and the search about learning more creative and effective strategies to market and sell to them.

In 2001, when Doug Gollan, Daniel Wade and Carl Ruderman launched Elite Traveler, they saw an interesting media opportunity. There were plenty of magazines with a circulation of 500,000 to over one million that were thick with ads for $25,000 rings, $50,000 watches and $2,000 shoes. Yet, when one dug into the main syndicated research studies that tracked who read these publications, the results were shocking. One major study, only surveyed households with a median household income (HHI) of at least $100,000. In other words, to be included, both household earners had to earn six figures combined. Over 100 magazines were tracked meeting that criteria, yet only two publications had a median HHI topping $200,000 (Departures and Robb Report). Most magazines had a median HHI of about $150,000. Another major study, which surveyed all readers regardless of household income, found the actual median HHI of readers was somewhere between $70,000 and $90,000. Depending on the research study, it was probably only one or two percent of the readers of most magazines could afford to buy the luxury products and services being advertised!

Elite Traveler's entrance featured just 100,000 copies, but with distribution to private jets they were able to generate a readership with a median HHI of $2.2 million, and an average HHI of $5.3 million. At the time of Elite Traveler's launch, Noel Mignott, the Jamaica Tourist Board Deputy Director of Tourism for the Americas, joked to Doug Gollan "Other publications boast they have millions of readers. You tell me you only have millionaires."

Knowing that the people who would be picking up Elite Traveler were rich, and would generally be on a private jet with other people who like them had short attention spans, Elite Traveler pioneered a multi-award winning short-form editorial format in the luxury lifestyle magazine category. It drew on the adage 'a picture is worth a thousand words' and used an oversized format to showcase pictorials of the top suites in the major destinations readers were frequently traveling to. A Super Rich reader could page through a story on the 'Top Suites of Paris or Los Angeles' and for the first time, in one place, actually see the interiors of various suites, some that rented for as much as $40,000 per night.

Instead of typical long-form stories with prosaic prose (such as, 'the sun appeared from the edge of the jungle on a misty morning') and self-serving features on star designers that were heavily pushed by their public relations people, Elite Traveler was short and to the point – sort of a luxury version of USA Today or Lucky. Instead of having just 800-numbers and websites, products or services that were featured included the name of a real person, with their email and phone number. If you saw a watch you liked, Elite Traveler gave you the number of a boutique that had that watch in their collection, and the name of the manager who could help you out. And with hotels, the magazine gave the name of the General Manager. After all, many of the Super Rich had lists of special requirements and bookings with adjoining and multiple rooms, which were too complicated for websites of the day.

Elite Traveler didn't just tell readers about the signature treatment at spas, it gave the name of the best therapist. Understanding that many of the Super Rich were self-made (something that many luxury brands hadn't actualized at that point), the publication included in its Top Suites stories of 'who slept there.' When they did reader research, the men always identified Elite Traveler for the pretty women on its covers (and a few ended up dating readers who tracked them down) while woman always talked about the beautiful jewelry on the models.

Readers liked the magazine, and Elite Traveler was able to track tens of millions of dollars in watches, jewelry and hotel suites that had been sold right off its pages, often sight unseen by a reader. The magazine was extremely successful. Within six years, it was generating $15 million in advertising sales revenue, and with nice profits.

Today, Gollan has moved on and last year launched a weekly "CEO-style" travel e-newsletter DG Amazing Experiences that reaches over 20,000 private jet owners worldwide, which enabled him to spend hundreds of hours closely researching UHNWs. Combined with meeting numerous Elite Traveler readers between 2001 and 2014, analyzing reader research, and spending many hours in conversations with marketers of luxury brands, led us to realize that Super Rich consumers were incredibly diverse, and often misunderstood by luxury brands and service providers.

We also understood there were some significant gaps between the research in the market, the strategies brands were using to sell to UHNWs and what we were hearing directly from Super Rich consumers. While many books interview CEOs and CMOs or large companies, we decided to go to the people who sell to the Super Rich every day, and hear from them directly about what works and what doesn't when it comes to getting more business from UHNWs.

In doing so, Gollan enlisted the help of his partner in launching Elite Traveler, Daniel Wade, and Michael Calman, who he had worked with during his tenure at Bergdorf Goodman and CitationShares, a private aviation provider.

In creating this book, we interviewed preeminent sales superstars of luxury who specialize in selling to Ultra High Net Worth individuals. The goal was to get out of the Ivory Tower and talk to those pros whose main focus isn't on focus groups, ad agencies, PR programs and complexities of managing businesses, but had extensive experience and direct contact selling to the Super Rich.

We hope their insights can provide you with a deeper understanding of the opportunities in gaining more share-of-wallet from the market of Super Rich consumers.

Doug Gollan
Michael Calman
Daniel Wade

August 2016

SPECIAL THANKS

To our sales superstars of luxury, whose enlightening and engaging interviews made this book possible: Marie-Lise Baron, Deborah Calmeyer, Bill Fischer and Stacy Fischer-Rosenthal, Henry Kim, Nick Linca, Deepak Ohri, Jon Omer and Stacy Small. And, many thanks to our interview transcriber, Zander Abranowicz.

To my parents David and Adele Gollan; my children Jennifer, Casey and Nichole; mentors and influencers Carl Ruderman, Richard P. Friese, Jerry Landress, Russ Prince, David Bernstein, Geoff Lurie, Dan Gibson, Susanne Samuelsson, Lisa Ahern, Greg Furman, the late Eric Friedheim and the great teams at Elite Traveler and Travel Agent, I have learned so much from and who inspired me over 28 years, and of course, the current team at Travel Market Report, the Mazzas and my good friend Anne Marie Moebes, who have offered me a great opportunity and enjoyment to be part of its Management Board. Thanks to the customers and partners who have invited me into their businesses, many who have become friends, and make what I am doing lots of fun, and to all of my friends who have been so supportive in helping launch DG Amazing Experiences and my other projects which excite me every day! Special thanks to Nicole Gurkin for her endless support and understanding.

– DOUG GOLLAN

To my wife Pamela and daughter Rebecca. And, I would like to the thank the great teams that I have worked with at Calvin Klein, Coach and Bergdorf Goodman, who collaborated on the development of extraordinarily creative products and customer engagement programs.

– MICHAEL CALMAN

To my wife Kelly, for her patience, love and unwavering commitment through 25 years of marriage, to my son Keegan and daughter Kyra who are a daily reminder of what is truly most important in life. Thanks to my mother Rita, my father Bill, Theresa, Mark and my extended family who have helped and supported me through the years. Thanks also to Carl Ruderman for his kindness, encouragement and generosity and to the mentors, colleagues and clients from whom I have learned so much.

– DANIEL WADE

INTRODUCTION

No matter where you are, there are Super Rich or Ultra High Net Worth (UHNW) individuals and families—that is, households with a net worth of at least $30 million. According to researcher Wealth-X, there are more UHNW families in Wisconsin, Maryland, and Minnesota—not combined—than there are in Russia. There are more in Ohio than in Saudi Arabia. If you're in the middle of the country, there are UHNW families in your area.

Despite representing 0.000029 of world population, by conservative estimates, the UHNWs account for nearly 20 percent of all fine jewelry, designer fashion, watches, fine dining, luxury travel and automobile sales. Depending on the research you look at, as much as 90 percent of the Super Rich are self-made. In other words, they grew up without luxury, and spent a good portion of their adult lives fixated on their businesses, not buying luxury loafers. Because they don't fit the stereotype, many luxury marketers are out-of-step about how to develop relationships, and how to effectively market and sell to today's Super Rich.

Estimates put the worldwide fortune of the Super Rich as high as $50 trillion, more than the combined GDP of the 15 richest nations in the world. Wealth-X reports they spend over $225 billion a year on lifestyle, from handbags to villas and everything in between.

While many think that the population of UHNWs are primarily from the worlds of Wall Street, Fortune 500 CEOs, royalty, actors, musicians, sports stars, or even Silicon Valley tech (although each sector comprises a portion of the UHNW population), many made their money on more mundane pursuits such as car dealerships, refuse collection, vitamins, farming, energy, real estate, services, construction and manufacturing.

Secrets of Selling to the Super Rich features interviews from 'sales superstars of luxury,' who have been on the front lines of ultra-luxury transactions spanning millions upon millions of dollars. These superstars share the misperceptions about the Super Rich, and now relate how their background, experience, knowledge and selling secrets have served to create extraordinary marketing opportunities.

When it comes to selling to the Super Rich, throw much of what you know about Baby Boomers, Generation X, Millennials and other demographic groups out the window. If you want to increase sales to the wealthiest consumers in the world, the Ultra-High Net Worth individuals, put away your broad brush. Many of the sales superstars of luxury interviewed for this book expressed that corporate marketing strategies often are not in sync with the Super Rich, yet at the same time, the Super Rich are influenced by media in much the same way as the masses.

One thing that makes marketing luxury products and services to the UHNWs difficult is that the Super Rich are not a homogenous market. What the Super Rich want may surprise you!

CHAPTER 1

SELLING FINE JEWELRY ON THE FARM

Interview with ... Jon Omer
VICE PRESIDENT, FABERGÉ

J on Omer is Vice President of luxury jewelry and watchmaker, Fabergé.
He has been a sales superstar cutting his teeth in Texas at Neiman
Marcus in the 1970's and then reaching the pinnacle of Ultra High
Net Worth selling for Italian jeweler Bvlgari, before leading the sales
effort for Harry Winston's launch of high-end mechanical watches. He
then led the North American sales efforts for Swiss couture watchmaker
DeWitt. From 2008 to 2012 he served as Chairman of the Board of the
American Watch Association.

What type of research would you typically do before you interact with new customers?

I start with a more basic approach. I simply Google the person, and whatever information comes up, I play off of that. Maybe I'm too old, but I'm not a big fan of social networking. I don't think you get a clear picture of the individual, what really drives the person. In selling to high net worth individuals, there are certain things you have to do. You have to—depending on the product—qualify their interest in the product. If you're selling sports cars, you have to know that the guy has always driven a Cadillac and that he couldn't care less about your sports cars. You have to understand where his interests lay.

According to research, there are less than 300 really genuine collectors of high complication watches in the United States. It's a staggering number because our population is so great, and the number of Ultra High Net Worth individuals among that population is so tremendous. They qualified watch collectors as men who own more than five watches. It's also a surprise, but it makes sense. Who are watch collectors? Those interested in high priced, ultra-complicated watches. It's a guy who's not only interested in the product, but who has the money and the will to spend on that product. That's why you have to get some kind of picture of what this guy's interests are.

Then, I try to find someone who knows the guy. The guys who buy these watches are known by a relatively small group of retailers around the country. The more information I can find out about him, the better off I am. I'm even better off if I can partner with someone who has some kind of relationship with him. More often than not that's a retailer.

Credibility is vital. You need to know what's important to the customer— what I call "credibility benchmarks." He may buy art, but doesn't see the worth in watches. He may buy property, but doesn't see the worth in buying sports cars. You need to find the driving interests and where he spends his money. Then you're much further ahead of the game.

Is the understanding what he spends money on, so that you could make a connection between the watch and, say, a sports car?

I would try to make that connection, but it doesn't always work.

Since I'm in the field of watches, I think we've taken a tremendous hit since 2008. In 2008, the world turned upside down. Men and women who had money began questioning the value of things. We have a whole new paradigm today. If someone is going to spend money on a particular item, they've set a mental benchmark as to what they would spend for a category. Today, $50,000 seems to be the ceiling for spending with non-collectors.

Someone once told me that Bill Gates wears a Timex. I don't know if this is true, but imagine if it is. Here is a man who can buy anything he wants, but it seems ultra-high-end watches aren't important to him. I've known other very wealthy men who wear Swatch, Timex, and other less prestigious watches. These men don't see the value in wearing a high end luxury watch. Someone asked me recently why Rolex and Patek have had the success they've had. Before the crash occurred, there were people who were spending money once a month on the next ultra-exotic watch. Richard Mille, Patek, a full slate of products. Some of them had as many as one 150 watches. The crash hit, and most of these guys took a financial hit. More than that, everyone began to question the true worth of certain items. Guys who really took the hit figured, 'I have these 30 exotic watches, so I'll sell them.' But there was no market. The makers of these exotic watches, although highly skilled and schooled, didn't have a commercial enough name to drive the resale value. The only brands that did—Patek, Rolex, Breguet—were safe, but from there you fell off the cliff.

Also, the taste level changed. If you were wearing a significant high end luxury watch before the crash of 2008, it was acceptable in many business environments. In the boardrooms (of financial institutions) after the crash, guys were told, 'Keep it low key, don't buy a big fancy watch, and don't flash your money. Everyone's watching us.' This mindset permeated the Ultra High Net Worth people here in the United States. We came from Puritans, and have always had a conservative vein, but I think the crisis reinforced that issue.

Have you had success converting the rich person who doesn't appreciate watches?

Never. Also, I've never had success converting someone who wanted to buy a Rolex, to buying something else. It's really strange. It's like Coca Cola. Pepsi has been trying to chip away at that brand name for as long as I've been alive. I use this metaphor: My grandfather used to take me down to the "big downtown" of Havana, Illinois. It had a John Deere dealership, a Chevrolet dealership, and a great bakery. We'd sit outside of that bakery and drink Pepsi. At some point, my grandfather decided that he liked Pepsi. Maybe he was a bit of a rebel. It's like Hertz and Avis—they have their brand locked into the mind of the buyer.

I've tried to convert people. I've spent money. I've traveled. I've gone to their homes. If the guy really likes you, and you've established a really nice relationship, maybe he'll come to you and ask you to find him a really nice watch. It'll be something classic—a Patek Calatrava or a really classic Breguet.

When you know that there is an interest in watches you can say, 'you know, the guy who designed your Patek now has gone into business for himself. Laurent Ferrier designed Patek's for 30 years, you should really take a look at his watches.' Why did he go into business? He retired and found that he didn't like retirement, so he decided to start his own company. He's doing things that weren't indigenous to the Patek brand.

The story is very important for any product, whether it's the carbon fiber chassis on a Ferrari to a wine that comes out of Bordeaux. The stories about these products are the hook. If you don't have the story, it's hard to invent one.

It takes about ten years to build a brand to where people recognize the name, even in today's age with marketing and everything. Richard Mille is a good example. They've been in the US market for about 14 years. Only in the last five or six years has the Richard Mille name attained good brand recognition for ultra-high end watch making. John Simonian, wrist watch entrepreneur and owner of Westime, Los Angeles, shared with me the story of his efforts in building the Richard Mille brand. He told me there was a period of time in the early years when it was nearly impossible to get a retailer to carry the Richard Mille brand.

You hear a lot about concierges, family offices. How important are the inter-mediaries in selling to the Ultra Rich?

Connections are everything. I'll use Rudy Silva as an example of a tremendously exotic watch. The retail price of this watch is $280,000, and the company makes 10 to 12 watches each year. For me to even begin a conversation with someone about a Rudy Silva I have to have credibility in front of that person. That credibility comes not only from jobs I've had, but also from the people introducing me. Most of these Ultra High Net Worth people, you can't even get to them. So unless you have an introduction, forget it. You're probably never going to touch them. Most don't make a habit of walking into stores to shop. They have people who insulate them from the daily running around that most people do.

So in order to get to them, it's a little difficult. They may, for example, attend the *Robb Report* selection of the Car of the Year to drive these cars. It's something they can't really buy, they can't collect them all in one place, and so they'll go to the event just to drive the car. They may end up actually buying one, and if you're there, they'll come by and say hello, and you'll meet guys you'd never otherwise see. And on the other side of the spectrum, there are guys who are ultra, ultra-wealthy who don't try to isolate themselves. They're just sort of ordinary guys. They still go to Kmart or Whole Foods to shop with the family. They play the lifestyle in the home; they usually have beautiful homes. They play it a bit in exotic cars; maybe they have a McLaren instead of a Ferrari, or a Pagani instead of a Lamborghini. But they may not show their wealth in the way they dress, or even in the choice of a favorite restaurant. It's really a mixed bag, so it's harder than ever to identify these people.

Once you've sold a very expensive watch, what type of follow-up or relationship building do you do?

If you sell it, it transcends the normal arena of sales. Nobody is going to spend that kind of money with you unless they feel you are one of their "go-to" people. They trust you. They've spent this money with you. If you're smart at all, build on that relationship. If anything, I've found that they're pretty loyal.

Does advertising work with the Super Rich?

I think marketing today is really a mixed bag. Where do you put the ad? What do these people read? How do we know what they read? We make guesses—we know that they travel by private jets, or by yacht. They have to buy gas for that private jet or yacht someplace. So we begin to form a picture of how we can touch them. Would I put an ad in an Elite Traveler magazine, or a high fashion magazine? Probably yes, because they fit the profile and lifestyle of the Super Rich individual we are targeting. When does he read a magazine? When there's no distraction, and when he's relaxing on his jet or yacht. Or maybe he's in a hotel waiting for his wife to get dressed and he picks up a magazine from the coffee table and leaf's through it.

By and large, print media has taken a tremendous hit over the past six or seven years. But, it's still necessary. Age has a lot to do with this. Young people are not reading print newspapers and print magazines as much as the 45 plus age group. But, that 45 plus age group has the most money. So you don't want to dismiss print media.

How does advertising function in your industry?

It's reinforcement. About four years ago I was working with DeWitt, and we did an experiment with our marketing budget. DeWitt is a high end luxury watch company, but was a relatively unknown brand. We wanted to spend about $500,000 in a marketing push to raise brand awareness. We could have spent this in four different markets, or most of it in one market. We chose the latter, and the market we chose was the US. Most high net worth individuals read US publications, no matter where they live in the world.

The following year, a company was doing a watch brand recognition project, interviewing high net worth individuals in different key markets around the world. They would ask people what watch brands they recognized from a list of brands they were researching, one of which was DeWitt. To our great surprise and delight, DeWitt was a name that appeared towards the top of the list of brands people recognized. This was after a year of heavy advertising. So we learned that this heavy up program actually was able to have a measurable effect in driving brand recognition.

Everyone talks about great customer service, but what is great service for your rich customer?

24-7 availability. When I give out my business card it has my personal cell phone number on it. I have people who call me, send me texts, at 11 or 12 o'clock at night. In today's world, accessibility and dependability are the two key elements in customer service. The worst thing that you can have is a customer with some kind of issue reaching your voicemail. These UHNW people don't want to walk into some shop with their hundred-thousand-dollar watch and some salesperson says 'well, it's going to be about six months before you see this again.' They want to deal with the top people, so top people have to be accessible.

Is that an advantage for smaller luxury companies?

Absolutely. They're intimately involved in every aspect of their businesses. But, larger companies are focused on making it an advantage also. He has a Twitter, a blog, etc. You can get to John Cruz if you want to get to John Cruz. Just call his secretary. And Sales Associates at Saks have direct access to him. That's the key today. Direct access, accessibility, and action.

How do you communicate with your customers?

It's critical. They don't want to read your emails. They get tens of emails per day. It sounds trite, but I'm leaning more and more toward direct phone calls, if you know the secretary, and there's a thing called the letter. If you were to handwrite a note or send a photograph of something, you'd definitely get their attention.

Two things happen when they get emails, and neither one of them are really good. Either they delete it without looking at it, or they look at it and it doesn't register because they're busy. Most executives I know look at their emails twice a day, once in the morning and once at night. If they have one hundred emails to go through, think about how much time they're going to put into it.

If you're talking with someone with some knowledge of watches, how much detail do they want about the watch, or is there such a thing as too much detail?

I had a great experience in the Summer and Fall of 2013. I worked in a high octane sales environment on the sales floor at Saks Fifth Avenue. Customers like to be romanced a bit, they like to know a little bit of information, but there is a point where you kill the sale by over-selling it, by telling too much. It's true with all people.

You have to remember what attracted you to something, whether that's a watch, a car, or a suit. It was the physical sight, the image of it. It looks good to you. And when you're making a sale you better believe that, and you better focus on it. It's fine to tell them, 'this comes from a guy who's the ultimate watchmaker,' but to start explaining how a double tourbillion works, you're wasting your time. Unless the guy asks you, 'well, how does this really work?' Ok, then you better know how it works.

But up front, what's attracted him? He's seen this watch, and 'oh my god, look at this thing! What does it do?' 'It overcompensates for the effect of gravity, which is so minute you'll never know it anyway.' But the way the thing works, the way it looks, and you have to focus on the aesthetics.

I have people who've bought tourbillions and they have no idea what they do. They don't care. They just like the fact that that little gizmo goes around the circle down there. It looks cool. The layout is perfect, the case is perfect, it's highly polished, and it's sexy.

Is there a difference between self-made and inherited wealth in spending behavior?

It's really a mixed bag. New wealth, or entrepreneurial wealth, will maybe be a bit more receptive to new products, whereas 'old money' tends to be a little more conservative and traditional with their tastes. The biggest challenge with the watch business today is reestablishing the value, the beauty, and the aesthetics of the watch business. We've got so many things going on today. We have cell phones telling us the time. And, Apple has come out with a watch.

The interesting thing about Apple is that they came out with a watch in three categories. They're following the traditional guidelines of establishing a watch brand: an entry-level product, a sport product, and a classic product. They researched many different watch brands to find out how they established their watches, and Apple has done the same thing with their watch. So the point is this: Apple is actually doing the industry a favor. They're refocusing the attention on a vehicle that rests on your wrist, and not something that you hold in your hand. That's a great starting point.

There is a traditional screen on the Apple watch. Why would they even have that? Because it's important. I find that very interesting.

Does the Ultra High Net Worth and their companies care about the watch industry's collaborations with philanthropic organizations?

When I was with Fred Joaillier, in 1978, we already had the game starting. We had customers coming in, saying, 'I'm on the board of directors for the Cancer Research Foundation, or St. Jude's Hospital, and we're having an event. Could you donate something?' These charities were smart. They realized that a client was going to have better access to that luxury brand than the guy from the cancer foundation walking in and asking for something. It's leverage. So it started then. It started in a 'genuine' way. The person was already a client, and you felt good as a company about doing something to support the client and support a charity event. I'm a firm believer that people with wealth give back. How this is maneuvered is sometimes interesting to watch. Do these people come back from that charity and buy from you? In my experience, not so many. The one who was your client stays your client, but does it help you gain you new clientele? Not so much.

Part of it is associations, also. If you have people in your organization who have friends, acquaintances, business partners, etc. who are involved in this charity, there's more likelihood that they might become a client. It all goes back again to personal relationships.

Let's talk about events. Art Basel Miami used to be a small event, now it's 75,000 people, and you have luxury brands tripping over each other down there trying to find maybe 1,000 UHNWs amongst the posers. From a salesperson's point of view, are they worth the investment companies make?

Unless I'm tremendously mistaken, these events are at best, exposures for the brand. I have personally, in my forty-six-year career, only made two sales at such events. I've probably done, conservatively, more than a hundred-fifty of these events. It's a branding exercise. Selling high end products has a certain intimacy to it. And that intimacy is negated by a big event like Art Basel. People go, they drink, they have fun, they enjoy themselves, but you lose the intimacy of establishing that personal relationship. There's too much going on.

If you're Bvlgari and you make a fun watch called "Art Basel" that retails for $500, you'll probably sell it because it's a fun, inexpensive purchase. If you're trying to sell the ultra-thin tourbillon for $140,000, there's probably less chance of that happening.

What type of interests have you seen among the Ultra High Net Worth?

'People with money' is such a broad sweep. An Ultra High Net Worth guy can be a guy who runs a crocodile farm in Louisiana who sells skins to

Hermés for their bags. He's worth all this money, drives a Ford F150, and for him, luxury is a new shotgun, or maybe a trip to Paris. Or, there's a guy who lives in San Francisco, maybe made his money in Silicon Valley, 31 years old, and he's read about all these places around the world. When someone makes a lot of money, they don't necessarily rush out to buy a lot of things, but one thing they do is travel. All the key cities in the world have their Rodeo Drives. You walk down any major shopping street in the world, you'll find the same brands, but travel brings the client to the brands. Travel is a key aspect of the life of anyone at any financial level. I'd imagine that you would find that a preponderance of luxury spending is done when people are traveling.

Do you pursue referrals? Does it happen? Do people not want their friends to have the same watch you sold them?

Referrals are funny. If someone bought something very special from you—and I've sold to everyone from Mexican Presidents to Middle-Eastern aristocracy to Japanese executives—I've never received a referral from any of them. Right now I'm doing business with a billionaire out of Hong Kong. They're in every social circle in Hong Kong, but I've never had a referral from him.

It goes back to accessibility. You become part of their private group, and that commodity has value. They want your expertise and your loyalty directed at them. They don't want to share you. It's almost like you work for them.

What about the relationship with the family?

They may share the family a bit, but the relationship is really one-on-one.

Tell me a bit about the sales cycle. Are there any ways to speed up the sales cycle?

Today, it's all about immediate gratification. One thing that speeds up a luxury sale is availability. It's ludicrous to do an editorial on a watch, then not have the product available. It's a killer in the business; it's an old world mentality. It may work for Hermés bags, but that's about all it works for. If you're a new luxury brand, and you catch someone's eye, you better be able to deliver. That's the first thing. The second thing that can speed it up is marketing saturation using multiple vehicles. It raises the awareness. The third is celebrity endorsements.

Perceptions play a great deal in the luxury game. If something is perceived as being a good product, people will trust it. If a company is perceived as being a good company, it goes miles in helping to sell their product.

When you have a product, the worst thing that can happen is you fall in love with that product as the person who's selling it. It blinds you to the buyer. You tend to focus on what to you are the obvious beauties of the product, but you don't listen to what the client is saying to you. A lot of people miss sales because they're so convinced or so indoctrinated by their brand that they think it's absolutely the best. If you listen to your client, you'll find what is important to them and you'll be able to sell to them. A big part of what we do has to be listening. It seems obvious, but I watch sales every day and it's not so obvious.

What about Customer Relationship Management (CRM) for the Super Rich person?

I start from the premise that we're all human beings. Someone feeling that you remembered them, and that they're important, is just as important to the rich guy as to the poor guy. I believe in sending a note—it could be one line—writing it out, putting it in an envelope, and sending it to them.

I have a good friend who was the head of Bozell & Jacobs for a few years. He used to do this religiously with all of the executives at Chrysler. We were talking once, and I asked him, 'what is the most important thing that you do?' He said, 'letting people know that I know what's going on in their lives and that I'm connected to them.' Looking at it in that way, birthdays and anniversaries and graduations are important landmarks no matter how much money you have. Can you think about the impact of getting a note in today's world instead of getting these online birthday cards?

What about spouses? How do they affect the sale?

I saw a salesperson blow a sale the other day. He was selling a beautiful Baume Mercier, not crazy expensive but a beautiful watch. The guy liked the way it looked, liked the way it felt. The wife said, 'honey, this is a great watch. It looks great on you.' The sales person didn't emphasize the positive input from the spouse, and focused on the negative hesitation of the guy, and lost the sale. If she had simply said, 'James, listen to your wife, how many times has she been wrong?' That's a win-win answer. If he says, 'well she's wrong all the time,' you could say, 'not this time!'

So humor is important as well?

I don't see as well as I used to. The little price tags are sometimes impossible for me to see. I look at them, and I say, 'excuse me a moment, I need my glasses because they're shrinking these price tags.' It gets a laugh, you show your human side, and let's face it, people want to buy from people that are human. So the more of your personal human side you can show, at least in the US—I'm not saying this is true for every culture—the better.

Speaking on the sales side, what have been the most effective and least effective corporate strategies that come to mind?

As things progress in the world, and the more we become more insensitive to human emotions and lose sight of interpersonal transactions, the more the human being wants that personal relationship. We need the touchy-feely communicative experiences. We're built for them. When companies fail to capitalize on the value of building interpersonal relationships—not through a cocktail party—maybe you have an intimate dinner party, and the owner of the company is there, and you have a conversation around the table, maybe not even about the product, just talking. This, in my opinion, in the future, will be the difference between selling to the UHNW and not. Is the CEO's ability to reach out and honestly discuss with potential customers still there? Get an honest feedback, get an honest opinion, provide a service at 3:00 in the morning.

So big brands, if they want to get Ultra High Net Worth business, have to have a sub-marketing strategy?

You can't have these services for the mass market, but you have to for UHNW. I'm going to use the word 'entitled.' People who've worked hard to earn their money and who are perpetuating it, feel a certain amount of respect is due them. You may call that entitlement, but if you want to keep this client you better be aware of it. If you recognize that, give the client a special way to access things, in a personal way.

Wealthy people know Tiffany's, Cartier, Harry Winston as brands, but do they know the specific products?

Some people don't even know what those brands are. They don't know how to pronounce them or they feel awkward saying them. European brand mentality is—you should know who we are. American mentality isn't that way. You have to flatter the client. 'Let me show you something that's the best of the best, knowing your taste.' Speaking down to people never works. Lifting them up to your level always works.

Anything more to add?

In selling, the answer 'no' does not exist. Elegance is not synonymous to luxury. Elegance is intrinsic. Luxury is manufactured. A rancher once came to me in overalls. He pulled out an advertisement page out of his back pocket. It was kind of soiled. It was a Piaget watch. 'Today is my anniversary, and my wife tore this page out of the magazine and left it lying on the table, obviously for me to find. Do you have this watch?' Ironically, we had the watch. He said, 'I think we have an account with you.' It was in the days when we had to call Dallas and they had to go through their card file. They found his name and said 'he can have whatever he wants.' He wore big overalls, a sweat-stained t-shirt, a straw cowboy hat, and cowboy boots. He'd been out all morning branding cattle on the range. He became one of my best customers, it became a relationship, I'd call him and say, 'hey, you've got an anniversary coming up, you want to buy something.' I'd ask if she'd been looking at anything. He said, 'Well yeah a couple of things. Come out to such and such side of the ranch tomorrow.' I'd drive out there, find him, sit on the back of a pickup truck, and show him necklaces. 'She's your wife, she's important; she's got to look great for The Cattleman's Ball.' That's selling at the level that we need to get back to. He's busy; he's running a ranch.

It goes full service to a client I have now. They wanted the product delivered to Hong Kong. That's what we need to do today to sell to the Ultra Wealthy.

CHAPTER 2
MAKING THE DUCK DYNASTY COME TRUE

Interview with ... Bill Fischer &
Stacy Fischer-Rosenthal
FISCHER TRAVEL ENTERPRISES

B ill Fischer may have invented the idea of that a travel agent could do anything you need. While other travel agents relied on airline commissions, Fischer pioneered charging well-heeled clients for his services. Together with his daughter Stacy Fischer-Rosenthal, they routinely arrange travel for Ultra High Net Worth executives, entrepreneurs, artists, and heirs. The fee to engage Fischer Travel is $100,000 and the company only takes a handful of new clients a year.

When somebody comes to you as a prospective client, what type of research do you do before you start talking to him or her?

Bill: They usually come recommended by our clients, so it's not as if we have to go out and sell them. They're pre-sold. We do check them out to make sure that they're the right client. They must be respectful. Just because they have a lot of money doesn't mean that they can walk into a hotel and cause a big ruckus. Over the years we've released clients due to poor behavior. We protect our reputation.

So talk about that—you're not jumping over hurdles to get new clients?

Bill: Certain times of year we can't take on new clients because we're too busy.

Stacy: When clients join and pay this amount of money they have a certain expectation. Bill and I have to look at our team's workload. Right now (before the Christmas holidays) we're working on average until 10:30pm or midnight, and then up again at 3 in the morning. It's peak season. Next week is crunch time. It's not as if clients leave on a trip and our work is done. Once they leave, the job really starts!

Bill: They have their own planes; they can leave and fly to wherever they want.

Stacy: They'll say, 'The weather's not good, we don't want to be on the yacht, get us a villa, we're fourteen people.' We accept the challenge and we deliver.

So how do you research the people who are coming to you?

Stacy: We read all the business pages to learn about their companies and net worth. We look online to discover their interests, social scene and causes they support. I think it's also a challenge. We have some new clients and are finding they are real micromanagers, which is ok, but we don't necessarily have the time for three-hour conversations, four times a week. Then, they'll involve me on a weekend. It's so labor intensive. I think, 'oh my god they're not even reading the itinerary! We've provided all the information!' But they're our client. So we perform our due diligence after a trip and say, 'you know what, I don't think this is a good fit.' But I cannot predict an outcome before working with people. Maybe they have difficult and overpowering personal assistants.

Are the assistants really delivering messages to the client?

Stacy: In the best case we manage the relationship directly with the client.

Are you meeting with clients in person initially?

Bill: Sometimes we meet them in person, sometimes over the phone. It depends on the client and where they're located; they might be in Europe or elsewhere.

Stacy: It's best when an existing client refers them, because we'll ask the existing client, 'what do they know about us?' And we'll know about new clients from our existing clients. They convey the relationship and trust that we've built over the years that the prospective client understands our power in the industry. These people approach us because they want the service, they'll pay for it, and they understand the 24-hour access, but won't be abusive about our time. There are so many layers to the relationships. We've found that the people who have read about us in the press or heard about us from an unrelated source don't always fit well. It doesn't happen that often because we really only take on about five new clients a year. That method has been pretty successful.

For your continuing clients, what would be the range of how much they might spend during the year?

Stacy: It depends. For a wedding or a special experience or a birthday party, it could be in the millions.

Bill: Just for that one event, for the hotel and the planes, could be in the millions.

Do you go out proactively and discuss upcoming events with clients, like a wife's birthday party? Or are you waiting for them to come to you?

Stacy: We have everybody's birthdays logged. We're constantly wishing people happy birthday, reaching out on anniversaries, birthdays, graduations, and major milestones to see if they want to plan something special. Sometimes they call to say, 'Please keep it on your schedule and follow up with me.' Or maybe they need help with a creative gift. We love that.

As an agency do you have CRM (Customer Relationship Management)?

Stacy: We have an agency-wide CRM. We collect everything we can on our clients. We use it for archiving information, what they liked about suites, dinner reservations, masseuses, tennis lessons, golf lessons, ski boot sizes or certain pros. The more information we gather on a client, the better, because it minimizes repetitive questions and enables us to work efficiently. We also have a list under every single client on the trip, what's open, what's pending, and so on. So if someone calls me, I know the dates, cancellation deadlines, money paid online, etc.

If someone's written up in the Post or the Journal do you add something like that?

Stacy: It does occasionally bridge into their personal lives—divorces, buying properties, or even requests for help with their development projects. They trust us; they know we know the players in the industry.

I'm sure you're privy to lots of interesting information about people. Have you ever been in a situation where there's a divorce and one of them doesn't want the ex-wife to use you guys?

Bill: Sure, it's happened. But it's also transpired where the client will advise us, 'it's ok for him/her to use Fischer Travel, and bill me!' It goes both ways.

Stacy: There are times when we say to the client, if there are children involved, that it's best to work with both of you, if you're splitting holidays. Maybe we'll separate it by assigning different travel agents. We are very discrete and take confidentiality seriously. If you don't want her or him to know about something, they won't.

Once they become a client, what are some things that you do to cultivate the relationship?

Bill: There are a lot of special experiences we create for the clients.

Stacy: I have a client headed to Japan this March, so I arranged a conference call with the client and our guide in Tokyo. The client mentioned that her son loves Pokémon and had asked if there was anyone who could teach him the Pokémon game. She just said it in passing, and we went on to other things. After the call I thought, 'Why don't I look if there's a Pokémon instructor in New York City?' It turns out there is, so on Saturday this child is going to the Nintendo Store and meet two instructors who will teach him the whole thing. The client was amazed because we listened to her and delighted her by following through on the details.

In another instance I attended the opening party at the new Park Hyatt in New York and saw their outstanding spa. I instantly thought about clients who schedule massages every weekend and love a couples' treatment room. The next day I called the clients and told them about the new spa and couples room. I now have it booked for a ninety-minute treatment with two therapists every Saturday the clients visit New York. They're delighted, because they didn't ask me for it, but I knew that this was something they enjoyed, and every now and then they'd call me at the eleventh hour asking where they could get a massage together. They love it and we've got it booked through January.

Do you find yourself socializing with clients?

Bill: Yes, from time to time.

Stacy: We do support their charities. They're all involved in giving back to something. We like to support their efforts and attend their charity events, where we have a chance to talk face to face. We want to show that we appreciate their business and know that they're doing good for mankind.

Does Fischer Travel have its own charities?

Bill: A couple of weeks ago I attended an event for Meals on Wheels at the Plaza Hotel. The women's leadership team invited men who donated $10,000 to come a women's lunch. I sat next to Blythe Danner, who invited me to see her on Broadway a few days later.

Stacy: As a company we participate in the Making Strides Breast Cancer Walk in Central Park and hired two student workers from the Cristo Rey School in Brooklyn. We also support Ramapo Children's Camp and Memorial Sloan-Kettering Cancer Center.

So it's more for you, not to impress your clients, because they have their own charities?

Both: Right.

After a trip is booked, what's the standard follow-up?

Stacy: We're constantly checking in with general managers, butlers, hotel staff, and yacht captains. We monitor everything. We don't want anything to escalate. Sometimes we'll hear certain things from staff that the client won't share. We receive emails from vendors about what the clients did each day. We consider ourselves part of the trip, and that's what I look forward to. But if the weather isn't great, and they aren't happy about this or that, we'll reach out, acknowledge it, and see what we can do to make it better tomorrow. So we're always in contact. When they're traveling it's harder than before they leave, though.

We're belong to several hotel boards which enable us to pass the perks onto our clients. We regularly upgrade accommodations, but sometimes they don't want to be upgraded. They want a certain type of suite because that's what they prefer. And we'll advise the hotel manager, 'Don't move them! Even if it's to the Presidential, because they prefer the Royal.'

Is price ever an issue?

Bill: Sometimes, but we know how to handle any difficulties. We have a client who owns a hotel, and we booked him to another location over the holidays. He asked us if we could sell his villa on his resort for the time he went away on vacation. And we did, for $35,000 per night, with a ten night minimum. It's not the price, it's the quality.

Stacy: But the purchasing client will say, 'it's a ten-night minimum at that kind of price point, and we're on a yacht before, so we won't use it for ten nights.' So, it's three days of back and forth between the powers that be. Finally, one party caved and we reduced the number of required nights at a higher price, so both clients were happy. It's not as if the clients are spendthrifts and say, 'no problem I'll pay you the full price for a two-week minimum.' They'll negotiate, but we're talking about big numbers.

Bill: It's a quarter of a million dollars for the stay.

In marketing it's all about segmenting, millennials, psychographics, and that sort of thing. Do you segment your clients by age?

Bill: We don't. We're now responding to the children of clients, but since they have been raised in wealth they don't follow the trends of other millennials.

Stacy: The children grew up with our service, which is really great. They have an appreciation for our work because they've always travelled this way. We've sent them gifts their whole lives, and have set up little things that would make a difference. Should they enjoy tennis, we'll set them up with a pro. If they like soccer, we'll arrange an introduction to players on FC Barcelona when the client travels to Spain. As they're getting older and becoming adults and getting married, we're planning their honeymoons. Most of them are in the position to be able to travel and appreciate a certain lifestyle. People want to have fun experiences, they want to feel young, and they want to be in all the hot spots on Earth.

And after the trip?

Bill: We'll talk to them to hear their likes and dislikes and take it from there.

Stacy: It's a conversation, and the more information they give us, the better we can serve them. We'll talk, meet or some clients will write detailed emails about the restaurants, or their feelings on different hotels. Maybe they loved this palace but didn't love this hotel. We listen to everything. Sometimes when we hear no news that can be an indication of good news!

Do you see a difference between self-made vs. inherited wealth?

Bill: As long as they spend the money! Not really. People are people, and it doesn't make that much difference.

What are some unexpected events and destinations for the Super Rich?

Bill: The World Cup is very popular. The Olympics are always a hot ticket.

Stacy: Clients in their 40's to mid-50's are very active. Surfing in particular has become very popular. At the moment it's huge. For example, I can think of six clients where this has morphed into a passion. They're flying off to the best waves several times a year. They not only want to hire a surf pro on-site, but they may also find an expert and bring them along anywhere in the world. Having a pro involved ensures they're not just surfing from the shore, but taking a boat out to deeper water and bigger waves. Also, the surfers are always in search of the best conditions. For instance, I'll hear 'I want to go to Costa Rica.' Then I'll arrange a trip, and they call me to say, 'oh, the swells are actually in Cabo!' And if Cabo's closed, well then, 'no it's actually in Nicaragua!' Between the weather and the waves, it could turn into fifty trips together. They have their own planes, so they're not held back by any schedule! I am seeing how restless our clients are. They're not happy just sitting on a beach. They want to stay fit, whether that's with extreme water sports, or a guy's vacation involving an extended biking trail. We'll arrange bike guides and chase vans. There are also clients who take their young children on the back of the bike because they'll see so much, or stay at luxury hotel at night, but during the day they're on the bike. We also stay on top of every unique event involving art, wine, and food.

Bill: We sent a whole group of friends on a truffle hunt. First of all, they let us know a month before. Every accommodation was reserved a year in advance. So now we had to find someplace. We knew someone whose brother owned a hotel, but there were people staying there, so we bought them out. We also paid to have the villa finished in time to bring the group in. Eleven guys. Hundreds of thousands of dollars.

What about major events that attract your clients for weekend trips?

Stacy: The Final Four basketball tournament is sought by our clients with kids. The Super Bowl is obviously huge. We're always proactive and hold rooms in advance for clients because we don't know which team will play and who'll be interested.

Bill: We do the same with Disney. It's a big item for our clients with families. They can enjoy something like a Segway scavenger hunt where characters will give them clues along the way, to an exclusive experience that can run sometimes hundreds of thousands of dollars. We've also we've opened the park for our clients to visit privately.

Stacy: As an example, we had a client staying at the new Four Seasons in Orlando with their 8-year-old son. There's a cartoon dog names Bolt and I overheard one of my agents say that they're flying the actor who dresses up as the "official" Bolt character from Los Angeles, to greet the child and create a special memory.

Any other unusual requests?

Stacy: One client was hosting a costume party and wanted me to arrange costumes from the Edwardian era for the families attending, in a Downton Abbey style. I was reading Entertainment Weekly on a plane I saw that Susannah Buxton, the costume designer from Downton Abbey had just retired and was pursuing other opportunities. So, I emailed my assistant and said, 'get in touch with this person.' She got in touch with Susannah's manager, who did a double-take and asked 'a costume party in someone's home?' We asked if she had access to the Downton Abbey wardrobe. We told her the party was in two weeks. She said yes. The client told us, 'do it.' So Susanna's in London, the client is in Long Island and we put it all together. We arranged two business class tickets, a luxury hotel in New York, car services, food, and x amount of money. Four trips back and forth. The tailoring, the makeup, the accessories, the dressing. Talk about money! The clients were blown away. Friends of mine attended the party, and I asked, 'how were the costumes?' They replied, 'oh my god can you believe they got the costume designer from Downton Abbey?' And I said, 'oh really?'

Here's another one. An agent received a call on a Wednesday from a very selective, high-end client. His birthday was Friday and he wanted to go to Duck Dynasty to celebrate. I happen to know someone who imports more duck than anyone else to restaurants. I thought Duck Dynasty was a Chinese restaurant! So I asked an agent to make a reservation at Duck Dynasty. She comes in and says, 'What are you talking about? It's a reality TV show! You've never heard of it?' So we found the manager of Duck Dynasty's duck calls warehouse, arranged a visit for the client to create a customized duck call, and even finagled a "roadkill lunch" cooked and served by Ms. Kay.

Bill: You'd never think that these sophisticated people would want to go down to Louisiana to eat roadkill.

Stacy: In two days and fifty thousand dollars later, they got their wish. They made their duck call, met the family, and had a "road to table" lunch. I have the producers of Duck Dynasty calling me every week asking what more we can do!

Is this person also on the boards of museums?

Both: Yes, yes.

Bill: We have people who live uptown who ask us to book them somewhere downtown for the weekend, for the different experience.

Is the Duck Dynasty situation rare?

Bill: Whatever they want, we'll get it for them some way or another.

What about drawing the line?

Stacy: If it's illegal, we won't do it.

Bill: If this is what they want and they'll pay for it...

Stacy: A client wanted to plan a getaway birthday party for his 80-year-old father, a former golden gloves boxer. The client wanted a professional boxer to knock on his father's hotel room door and wish him a happy birthday. So I thought, maybe we can make this more of an experience? I was thinking of calling George Foreman, and so on. But then I thought, what about Don King, because he's a personality? So we talked to Don King and he agreed to do it. With our help, the client flew his family to the hotel, celebrated at dinner and had Don walk in with the cake. Don King attended the party and took pictures with everyone! The father wasn't in great health and would travel to the Mayo Clinic the next day, so I had the picture of him, his son and Don King framed and placed in his room when they got there.

When you look at the generic travel research, it says that the wife influences the travel decisions. Yet if you look at UHNW for the most part it's the husband—most UHNW are male.

In this segment of affluence, I find that many decision-makers are men, but I genuinely look forward to the day when we serve more women who reach positions of great wealth. Also, in planning trips, I can say I've interacted with husbands and wives back and forth to make the trip they both want.

Do you do any special outreach to the intermediaries like the personal assistants?

Stacy: Sure, we'll take them out to dinner and give them birthday gifts. When they're happy, we're happy. They're a big part of the equation. We don't want them to feel threatened, we want work together with them and perform as a team, so that their boss and our client are happy. They can be a bit intimated because we're pretty strong-willed and inquisitive, but it's because we want to be on the same page.

Are there any other things you think would be interesting?

Bill: What they want is for us to be able to get whatever they can't get. It's not about price, it's about executing the impossible.

Stacy: It's also about their time. Everyone's so busy. They want to spend time with family and friends and be confident there's a seamless travel experience ahead. We also make sure they're getting the best, and what they want. My clients don't have time to research, plan and manage their travel. They leave it up to the experts. That's why clients come to us and say, "I just can't do it anymore." The clientele is very well-read, worldly, and sophisticated. They say 'we have the means, we need you.'

If you want to become a client of Fischer Travel, how do you do that?

Bill: First we talk with them and determine if we're right for one another. Then it's $100,000 to start, and $25,000 per year to stay on, and additional fees on top of that.

Anything else you'd like to add?

Bill: There's another thing every day that people want, you never know what it's going to be.

Stacy: We scored a same-day reservation at Peter Luger for six people at 7pm. The client arrived without a debit card or cash. As you know, Peter

Luger only accepts cash. I receive the distress call while sitting at my desk. Bill was about to leave the office and meet his driver when I asked him to make a detour to Brooklyn. So Bill walked in with a wad of cash and handed it over to the client. The client immediately called me and exclaims, 'How awesome is that? King Fischer walks in here and pays for my dinner!'

On the day before Thanksgiving the same client called us asking for a private chef because he invited fourteen people over. We made it happen.

Last Saturday, another client's chef had walked out on the job and he asked if I could reserve a table in the Pool Room at Four Seasons for that night's dinner? Even on a Saturday night in December, with our relationships, it's no problem.

It's all about doing something that money can't buy. It's relationships. Bill cultivated them, and we cherish them.

CHAPTER 3

MISSION: PRIVATE JET MAKEOVER

Interview with ... Marie-Lise Baron
PRIVATE JET INTERIOR DESIGNER

The business of designing private jet interiors isn't just an expensive one for the buyer, it is a personal one for the designer. In addition to working with the jet owner, a designer works with family, flight attendants, pilots and others in the inner circle of the Ultra High Net Worth. It involves numerous group meetings and one-on-ones. Changes can be costly, so making sure the designer delivers what the owner actually wants, versus thinking what he or she wants is critical. For each change, there are also many engineering studies to do, and many security limitations to respect the law. Marie-Lise Baron has made her mark spending countless hours with Super Rich private jet owners, their families, flight crews and support teams, to help bring their visions for their private jet interiors to reality. Offering talent, fidelity and integrity, the international designer Marie-Lise Baron, succeeds with grace in naturally to harmoniously match both the masculine and feminine elegance in details, functionality, ergonomics, and the choice of precious materials, with very high care on completion service and quality control. Most of all, her determination and loyalty, together with high intuition ability in understanding and meeting each person's needs and aspirations, allows her to offer a unique and personalized art creation for each customer. Her personality, unique talent and dedication to each project, make her a reference, a person and a designer that one and all can fully trust.

In your role as a designer of private jet interiors, you're working directly with jet owners?

Yes, I do, and I also design yachts, residences, offices, commercial projects and international special events for different companies. I also produced a commercial movie and many other projects as the design director for an international transport broker from Italy, one of the most important companies in the world. I had many other requests; design cloths and cars interior improvement for a specific customer. So I'm more than a private jet designer, I am a design director and provide design for many other owners requests. I have to work directly with the owners to make sure I understand their needs and bring them in the right direction, to respect the exact vision of their entire projects.

And that could be houses, offices, yachts?

Exactly, and more. I also work with the most important and luxury international real estate agency of the world.

How do you prospect for clients?

I take careful care of my network and I keep my contact with those people very closely, with a lot of respect and privacy. I never tell anyone the name of my customers, and it is one of the most important things to respect. Nice relationships can be born from some of my projects. Example, I have such a nice relationship with one of my clients, their family and the crew, that they invited me to leave with them in their private jet to go on vacation. We became friends, so they have brought me very close to their private life, their kids; and I kept the business relations with the pilots, the family, and the crew. I was told this was the first time that the family had invited someone from their exterior world, and I was really touched by this statement. It's unusual, and I feel very honored to have this privilege. First of all, I see the heart and moral values of people. This is the way I treat my customers. I am naturally very interested by their career path, I am also very touched to hear their stories and how they reached their goals. Positive reputation and nice words-of-mouth are the most important ways to have clients.

So as you look at your clients, quite a few of them come from humble backgrounds. How did they make their money?

I work with people from all over the world; they come from varied backgrounds, cultures and countries, so of course their needs and behaviors are varied, as well as their success stories. Some of them come from very poor and humble families, and they always keep the human aspect throughout their lives. Some of them inherited family money, others went to school, had an ingenious idea and worked very hard to make a success of it. Some of them are part of a family owned business that have been in their families for over five generations.

During the course of a year, how many projects are you working on?

If I work for a company, for example, a manufacturer of private jets, I can have ten or more private jets at the same time at different stages of completion. But, if I work as a private consultant, like I do now, it is most important to be available when the customer needs me. Have just one jet or yacht at a time, maximum two is perfect for me, never more than that. It is very important for me to feel comfortable with the customer and the project, and I choose all of them very carefully. One year I received three offers, by three different customers, from two different countries, and of course I wanted to do all of them. I sent a contract to all of them, but I accepted just one of them. The only customer I signed with was the one that accepted my own terms. During the negotiations of the contracts, by coincidence, one of them required me to be in Montreal one specific day for a seat-check, and the second customer required me to be in US for a veneer inspection the same day. I was in a situation that I had to choose and accept only one customer. Those customers have a big crew to manage and I really don't want to say that I am not available to a customer. I work 200% on my customer's project, so I accepted only one contract. One of the nice parts of my business that I enjoy, is that I can actually choose and decide which client I accept to work with.

So they expect you to be there when they want you?

It is much easier for me to be available for the customer than the opposite. There are a lot of people involved when a meeting is called – the family, the pilot, the flight crew, the lawyers and more. So that's why sometimes I have to refuse other offers, to give 200% elite service to my elite customer. At the end of a seat-check, we went to a lunch, and I was sitting in the car with the client. He said, "Marie, I have a big question for you. Do you have a lot of projects at the same time with my project?" I said, "No, I am 200 percent for you." He said, "Marie, that's exactly what I want to hear." From my experience, it's not a good idea to have 20 different projects going on. They deserve and expect that you're giving 200% service with them and more.

When you're talking with potential customers, how long does it take from the time you initiate contact to when they hire you?

It takes around a year and a half, or two years to complete A to Z, a new aircraft. It depends; some aircraft need only renovation or cosmetic transformations, so the process takes less time. It depends on the changes we have to do, and the complexity of engineering and design.

And from the first time you talk to them, to the time they hire you?

Sometimes they've already bought the plane and they are ready to hire an external consultant. Some are looking to buy a new plane and are looking to set up the crew to work on the plane. Sometimes, there is a contest and customers want to meet many designers. Some of them know exactly who I am, they hire me and there is no question. When it's a new external reference, it usually it takes a few months.

How much are your customers spending on the planes?

In terms of the entire jet, from the beginning to the delivery, it depends on the company, the serial and the details of design. Each company has their own standards, specifications and options they offer. Some of the jets I designed start at $45 million, and can reach over more than $65 million. In the case where the customer hires me as an external consultant, my services are charged separately from the aircraft. The external designer is also hired to take care of all the details of loose equipment, cushions, blankets, bedding collection, glass collection, tableware, tablecloth, logos on items and every single important accessory and details. The best cashmere in the world for blankets can cost $1,500 per yard for the raw product, even before I start the high end product. The loose equipment is charged separately from the professional service, and the price of loose equipment depends on the design, the collection, the choice of material and quantity of items. In my practice, I inspect every order for approval, I make sure the customer saves money and receives exactly the ordered items. I am very rigorous, and this is how I work to give elite service to elite customers.

How do you charge?

There are possibilities to charge my fees per hour, or per contract. I have to evaluate the needs, how many hours the project is going to take approximately, and the type of the customer's requests, expenses and traveling needs. The terms of agreement are also very important for me, to accept and sign a project.

Do you try to find out as much as you can about them before you contact them?

Definitely, and that's a very important step. I have a ritual before I meet each customer. First, I gather information about the story, the culture, habits, interests, preferences of the customer I will meet. This is the best way to have a perfect meeting.

Do you use the Internet, Google?

I use common contacts first, and I complete my research on Google to be more familiar about the culture of each respective customer, and read a few publications on their story. That's the kind of research I do. I use my personal contacts and I Google.

Can you talk a little bit about your contact with the clients during the projects? Do you work directly, or with intermediaries?

It depends on the customer and the culture, but usually I talk and work with everybody. It depends on the stage of completion. Some of customers are not accessible, have someone responsible for their private jets, and in this case I talk and work with the crew. In the most common situation, the customers want to meet me and work directly with me. They want to trust the person working on their private jet. Most of my customers, I'm dealing directly with them.

By phone, email, combination?

It's a combination of many kinds of communication. First step, there are my calls and emails with their representatives, and then we plan a meeting with the client. Once the project is started, we continue the project with the same communication. I also use the mail to send samples when it is necessary. It depends on the stage of the project. When I work on the layout, master seat or materials approvals, I work with the jet owner and the crew. To work on the galley layout, I need to communicate with the flight attendants, or the owner's wife. Some of customers don't have any flight attendants and they like to take care of this part themselves. For the stage of inspection, I work and communicate directly with the completion team to write my report.

But they're going to nice hotels, buying expensive watches and jewelry, that sort of thing?

Yes, it is the kind of pleasures they can afford. Some people are buying expensive items when there is a significant event, like a marriage, anniversary, vacation; and for some of them, it is a lifestyle. Items can be expensive for their brand, some for their high quality, some for their rarity, or as a unique item of collection. The consumer habits are different for everyone, it depends on the backgrounds, cultures, tastes and personality of each.

What type of gifts have you received from clients?

I never expect a customer offers me gifts or invites me somewhere and it is not the goal. During a project, it is very important for me to stay objective and professional, but it is always appreciated when a customer show me his gratitude. I always wait when the project is finished, as a private consultant, to accept gifts if they want to offer me a gift. I never accepted a gift in the situation I work for a company. So on a private consultant status, at the end of a project and many months after, some gave me few gifts to thank me and show me their gratitude; wines, vacations, but when they invite me to spend time with them, that's the most beautiful gift of gratitude.

After you've done a private jet for somebody, are you typically staying in touch with them afterwards, or are you waiting for them to contact you? Have you received references?

I received many references from words-of-mouth, but stayed in touched with one customer and family. This is a very special person, a special family for me. We had a very special contact and they welcome me at their house. The pilot told me "you're the only one who can stay at their house"—for me that is such a privilege and they welcome me in such a private field. When a customer lets me take pictures in their private home, they trust that the pictures will never go anywhere. For all those reasons, this is why I keep a very long friendship with the family and keep in touch together. I will go to the city at this time of year and we'll arrange for a time to meet and spend some time together. They invite me, and for me it's always a privilege. We became friends naturally, and I am very protective of their privacy.

So obviously you get to know these people fairly well, what are their interests? Golf, sailing, hunting, fishing, opera, art?

I can say about few of them. Golf, soccer, wines, restaurants, cars, yachts, houses, architecture and highly organized trips. I can say cars and trips are the most popular for men. Very high quality and special design shoes and clothing are also popular. One of them owns a golf club for his pleasure and welcomes his friends. You can land with your helicopter on his golf club.

Is the close relationship you enjoyed with that particular the norm, or is it an exception?

It's an exception. Usually it's only business, but this one is more than a customer. It's a family relationship, like with the crew and the family. I also kept friendship with few employees.

What is your relationship like between the jet owner and the crew?

It has to be very professional. It is possible to become friends and talk about friendship only when the project is completed. When we're working on a project it's really business, professional and I am very clear on that point. There is nothing other than work. There is a limit to respect with the crew and customers. In this field, it's very easy to lose a reputation and the trust. It's very important that those professional limits and rules are respected, to be able to stay in the high level of this field. In the private aviation field, it's easy to know if someone made a mistake and know the reputation of somebody. It is also better and safer to choose neutral topics for discussions.

So it's a very small circle?

Oh, yes. The earth is only one world for international famous business people and travelers, and all the people who serve them around the world. They have to communicate together constantly, and share different and important information between each respective crew of the customer, to provide the best elite service and protection for elite customers. A privacy agreement is always signed to protect ultra-private customer's information and security.

How important are the pilots and the flight attendants in the process of design-ing a jet? Are they influential on the owner?

They have to be informed of every single detail of owner's habits, tastes, requests, and what he or she likes and doesn't like. Each of them also have their own needs to reply very quickly to customer's requests. They share very important information with me to plan the design of the gal-ley, the crew cabin, the cockpit materials, and the entire jet. One of the pilots I worked a lot with, arrives one hour before the customer, to make sure that everything is perfect, as per customer's tastes and expectations, and to avoid delay if there are a few unexpected events. This customer's time is the most precious thing in the world.

When you're working with the owner of the jet, are most of them interested in the detail, or mostly the big picture?

Designing a private jet involves a lot of details, and they care about every single detail. If I bring new ideas to make sure that they're more comfort-able, they appreciate that. They like when I can increase their comfort through details, and when I bring my input about that. They appreciate that kind of experience and open personality.

When they come to you, do they have a color scheme in mind, pictures of other jets, pictures of furniture, things like that?

They have their own tastes like everybody, and they never bring anything to my meetings. First, they provide verbal information on their taste. Based on my experience, the first scheme is always the one they will choose. Because I listen to the customer very carefully, and because of my experience, the first scheme is always the best idea I came up with. I design two more for the customer, but usually, the first scheme is the one they choose. Sometimes we mix the schemes together because the customer prefers one item in the first and something else in the other. We work together for the best.

And how about the spouse's involvement?

Sometimes the wife is present, and sometimes she is not. It depends on the function of the aircraft. If the function of the aircraft is centered with the family, the owner introduces his wife in the meetings. Her needs are highly considered and very important in the process. The colors, the textures, the family habits and design needs are a part of discussion. This part of meeting is very important for me, and the spouse needs to feel very comfortable with me. After the layout and technical meetings with all the crew, the owner and his wife, I have another meeting alone with her to work on choices of fabrics for pillows, cushions, throw rugs and all the bedding and loose equipment. Women care a lot about the comfort of the family. Sometimes when the jet's functions are for the family and the business at the same time, we have two sets of throw pillows and throw rugs for two different looks. I design a masculine look and a feminine look to please two different needs, and sometimes we have to mix them; it works well and everyone's happy. My role is to make everyone happy.

They have two sets of pillows, one for when there's business and one when the families on board?

Yes, it's a possible customer's request. It depends on the function of the jet. If this is a multiple functions jet, for business and family, it's possible to mix both styles together, or have two separate sets for each function.

When you're starting initial discussions, do they bring you pictures from magazines, or hotels they've stayed in, and say I want something like this, or is it more of a conversation?

It never happened in my meetings. It's more of a conversation, my experience and my feelings. When I visit them I can see the style they like. It's very easy for me to feel the person, and it goes with the flow. I have been a designer for 30 years now, and they can feel my experience. I have an interesting story here for you. In one of my previous projects, a first designer started the design, and then I was selected to finish the design. The first designer chose a leather color for the seats of this customer. Of course I was continuing with the pre-selected color that the original designer had chosen because she told me that is what the customer wants. To my eyes it was not balanced with the veneer and visually so uncomfortable for me to mix the colors that were chosen. I wanted to change the color of the leather for all the seats to fix my visual discomfort, but at that stage of development it was not possible. After a consultation with my colleagues, I decided at least, to propose another textured rich color for the business area. The owner looked at me and said, "Marie, how do you know this is exactly what I wanted from the beginning?" I replied to him, "this color is the perfect business color for you, and it suits you very well." And he asked again, "How do you know?" Honestly, I felt it and it was so obvious for me. This customer also owns a winery, and that was the perfect color to honor his tastes and wine passion. Finally, I realized this customer never asked for the previous color that had been picked by the first designer.

After the delivery, during a meeting in the jet with the owner, he asked me "if you had to redesign the jet, what would you change?" I replied, "'the color of the leather of all your seats, except the business area." He replied ''I never asked for the color from the first designer, and when you proposed to me the new textured color, I was totally amazed by the exactitude of your choice." It is so important to listen to the customer very well, and pay attention to every important detail.

You mentioned the Grand Prix in Monaco—do you go to events to find new customers?

It depends where. I would go when it's in Monaco, London, US and India. I would go to special events specialized for private jets and elite traveler customers. There are a lot of those events in US and Europe. Most of the customers come from referrals and good words-of-mouth from pilots or my previous clients. I have been published in the most prestigious design magazine of Morocco, *Décoration d'Exception*. They published eleven pages on me, and my private jet design work is located between ''Hermès" and the "Grand Hotel de Paris." It's a very high-class magazine and those publications don't really bring new customers. It brings more curiosity about me and my work.

Is there anything else you'd like to add in terms of dealing with the families?

For me, the most important thing is bringing satisfaction in my work, is to see the happiness and comfort of the customer, and to bring his dreams to reality.

CHAPTER 4

CAN YOU SELL THE SUPER RICH WITH SOCIAL MEDIA?

Interview with … Stacy Small
PRESIDENT AND FOUNDER,
ELITE TRAVEL INTERNATIONAL

S tacy Small was a successful magazine editor, writing for publications such as National Geographic Traveler and Travel + Leisure. She was founding Editor of Elite Traveler, a magazine delivered to the global Super Rich aboard their private jets. After fielding calls from readers asking her for advice on trip planning, she decided there was an opportunity to serve the UHNW market. Beginning as an outside contractor for an existing agency, Small has built Elite Travel International (no relation to the magazine) into a fast-growing agency with over a dozen agents, focused on serving the well-to-do from Silicon Valley and behind-the-camera Hollywood. Her innovative use of social media has proven that yes, rich people do use Twitter, Instagram and Facebook. Of course, getting their attention for your postings takes building a relationship.

How do you find new Super Rich clients? Do you actively look, and if so how do you do it?

Anybody dealing with this circle of clients builds business through referrals, the same way that a high-level financial planner or real estate broker is going to. People at this level want to work with someone who their friends have had good experiences with or that they feel comfortable with, who understands their needs. I've had new clients call me and say either, "so and so told me to call you, but you should know that we're not in the same income strata as so and so," but then we start talking and find that it means that they want to spend $5,000 a night not $8,000 a night on a hotel room. So they're still at that high level, but even at that level they're always clear about how they fit in to their friends who referred them to me. But the five-star hotel customer isn't referring somebody who wants a two-star hotel. They're still referring people who want that five-star experience, but it's an inner circle of referrals. It's 90 percent of my business. The other ten percent is coming from potential clients' own research. They're looking online for people who've been written about in business publications. I was mentioned in *Forbes* magazine about three years ago about how to find the right travel agents, and I'm still getting people emailing me saying that we'd be a great fit. They're comfortable with that because it's written in a business context. A lot of people have never worked with a travel professional before, but when they read about it in a business context they feel comfortable reaching out.

We define the Super Rich as people in the 30 million a year plus income range, so they're flying to some degree on private jets. Are some of the referrals for not as wealthy friends?

I mean they don't all refer me friends in the 30 million dollars and up bracket. They'll send me families of five who fly private or first and business class over to Asia and stay in top hotel suites, everything done privately. I see what type of spending their doing. They're still doing a lot of spending on travel.

Once you get a referral or somebody contacts you, do you do any pre-discussion research? Do you use the Internet before you start engaging?

It's the first thing I do. A guy who emailed me yesterday, his name sounded familiar to me. I Googled it and it turns out that he's one of the top financial planners in a wealthy area of Pennsylvania. He graduated Syracuse University the same year I did and we have some mutual friends on Facebook. So I look for common ground to start the conversation. Nobody thinks it's weird anymore to Google someone or look on LinkedIn. Everyone likes a bit of background on who they're working with.

It gives me an idea of what their expectations are going to be. If it's the managing director of a major finance company I'm not going to worry about scaring him off with some of the costs of the suites or the private jets.

What's the core range of what people are spending?

For Christmas we have our biggest bookings, with four bookings over the $100,000 mark for families. The lowest spend would be about $40,000; $60,000 is basically what we're dealing with. That covers the hotel and some private tours. On one trip it was too much of a hassle to fly between two cities in Asia. So we contacted a local operator and for $48,000 got them a jet charter for a family of five. And you know what, it was a bargain. It's between Thailand to Bali. They didn't want to lose a day of travel, and they only have nine days for the whole trip.

What's the interaction with the client like? Personal assistants, gatekeepers?

Combination. Some of my top clients' assistants or gatekeepers are empowered to work with me directly, and for me to basically guide the decisions. They'll give me a sketch of what their boss wants, the destination or the dates they can go, or a couple of ideas. They're basically charged to work with me to put it all together. They'll check back, but some of them know their bosses so well that there's that trust. In other cases, some of the Ultra Wealthy clients like to deal with me directly, usually at night or on weekends. They'll loop their assistant in so they get the details, and I'll work with the assistants on the minutiae.

How are travel decisions made among the UHNW? Is it collaborative—what about spouses?

It's a real mix. I have a lot of clients where the wife will call initially, and we'll make some ideas and I'll give her information, but it'll come back to "let me check with my husband." Then we'll do a conference call to make sure everyone's happy.

Have you met most of your clients in person, or is it mostly over the phone?

No, we develop really nice relationships by email, by phone, or if I'm in a city where my clients are, I'll meet them. San Francisco, Boston, New York, Los Angeles. It doesn't seem to be important to them, though. They seem very comfortable by phone or by email.

What do you do to get them to buy more? What type of information do you track for them? Where they've gone, preferences, birthdays, anniversaries?

A big goal is getting better at that. The company's grown and we have more and more billionaire clients. We need to pass on information to the suppliers that we're working with. Nobody likes to be asked twice. We have a pre-trip form that my assistant sends out a couple of weeks before the trip. Food allergies, birthday, anything special going on while you're traveling; some good information to send to the hotels. And then the hotel has everything and it's up to them to execute once the clients get there. We keep as much information as we can on file. We use dapulse. There's an app on iPad and iPhone. It allows us to customize CRM (Customer Relationship Management). So if I get an inquiry, it gets posted on there. We can't afford to miss a beat with these clients. We also use AXUS itinerary management, a mobile app our clients really enjoy, as it puts their entire trip at their fingertips on their phone.

Once they're on the trip how do you monitor how things are going?

My clients are very tech-savvy. They're posting on Facebook throughout the trip. I can tell from the tone of the posts and the photos to make sure everything is going well. If someone posts, "that meal was terrible in Bangkok last night!" we'll ask the hotel to reach out. I do really try to reach out while they're away. It's a lot easier to do that proactively. But we also see that the clients' expectation is that we're present throughout the trip if they want to change the itinerary. It's how they live their lives at that high level. We work on the fly to make changes as the trip goes.

What about trying to get them to take extra trips? Do you reach out for birthday's, holidays, anniversaries?

Not so much for special occasions. They're usually pretty on that. But the reason I use social media so proactively is because it generates revenue, not because it's just really fun and I like to do it. I come back from a trip like Fiji, and a client says, oh we were trying to figure out where to where to go for my wife's fiftieth and that place you went looks amazing, could you tell us more about it?

Why don't you talk a bit about your social media strategy? What's worked, and what hasn't worked?

I was an early adopter of using social media. What that did for me was get me immediately connected to the founders of these social media companies and some of the execs and early employees who still work there. That's how I've initially been connected to some of my early clients who are up there in Silicon Valley. That's where they communicate. It was an experiment at the time to see who's using Facebook. I have friends whose husbands have really big jobs and travel really well and they didn't realize that they have a friend in the travel industry. So using tools like Facebook and Twitter to communicate, they see my posts from amazing trips I'm taking. They'll reach out and say we take a $50,000 trip each year at Christmas, and I've been booking direct, is that something you can help us with? It's a great marketing tool. It's free and I'm getting a lot of attention from people who didn't even know I'm in the travel industry. For the young billionaires in Silicon Valley and here in LA, Facebook is like their telephone. If I want something immediately I just message them directly on Facebook. Their assistants are on there. I'm posting photos not because they're pretty—I'm strategic about how I'm posting things. It's like a photo diary but I'm also posting information because I know that certain clients see that and more often than not they reach out and say put that on our list.

What aspects of social media have been more effective than others?

The debate in the beginning of Twitter was about whether the Super Rich were on there. All the luxury companies, all the fashion brands were backing away from it. That's until Mark Cuban, or Barbara Corcoran gets on there. All of my favorite entrepreneurs are on there using it as a way to talk to their audiences, so I use it as a way to engage with new potential audiences. It's a communication tool and a way to stay up on what's happening and read up on comments.

My following on Twitter is like 72,000. So I'm in a whole other league there. I continue to use Twitter to communicate with that bracket. I got one of my first Silicon Valley clients because an executive tweeted asking who has been to the Maldives, and where to go. I took a chance and reached out to him, and ended up booking a trip that became his engagement trip. I booked their European honeymoon a year later and they recently had their first baby. My clients are growing up, they have kids, bring nannies, need another room, so it moves them into another range of travel.

I do the business and the leisure travel for some of my top clients. When it's business, they're traveling with other people typically, so oftentimes they'll get a junior suite or a bedroom that they can use as a meeting room for the little group that's there. But everyone else is getting regular rooms. They'll say they don't need anything fancy. I hear that a lot. Even when it's just a couple, I'll book them the top suite to blow them away, and it turns out that they're not comfortable there. That's not really their style, or they would have preferred the junior suite that's less flashy and a little cozier. They can afford the biggest suite, but everyone has a style that they're accustomed to. On the flipside, there are some clients who are recently divorced or have a new girlfriend, and so now instead of being conservative about the way that they travel with their family, they're traveling more with private jets and asking me for the bigger suites and traveling more frequently.

What about price? Do they bring it up? If so, how do you hold the line if price is an issue?

It's funny. We don't say, "what's your budget," but we'll ask what's a comfortable range for this trip. I don't want to make them uncomfortable but I do need to know so that we give them the right options. Sometimes they'll say, "I don't know. Can you give me some options?" It's not about price usually but sometimes they'll just say it's just a weekend, let's not go crazy. But the big trips they do want to be special. The trips we're booking for next summer, family trips or birthdays, the wife might cringe a little but when they realize the price of a hotel on the Amalfi Coast, but then when I tell them that I was just there and how incredible it is, they'll be fine and say "book it." They just want validation.

But you don't have a lot of haggling?

Not really, but sometimes they'll ask about some unexpected things. They don't want nickel and diming. They want the high price to include everything they included. Don't charge for Wi-Fi, don't charge for a beach chair. That'll piss them off with the small charges that they expect to be included.

For your really rich people, do they care about special deals?

Maybe some of the younger ones who are on the Internet a lot and are sort of conditioned for bargains, they know that stuff is out there and will ask about promotions at certain hotels. Sometimes. But it's not a deal breaker. They'll appreciate it if it's there, but it doesn't drive the decision at that level.

You bring up an interesting thing, because you talk about how wealthy people today came from moderate means. A billionaire today, 10 years ago was sleeping on a couch. When they come to you, what's their experience level in terms of knowing what's out there?

Some clients have been working with me for five years. I had to be patient when my early clients said, "I don't want to spend $500 on a hotel room," and, "I don't want to fly business class." Then they'll stay a night in their first 5-star hotel on one trip, and start to fly business class. When they hit that point, they'll realize they really like it. They might say that they're not comfortable flying business class at the price of tickets now. They might say that they're fine going coach, because that's what they flew growing up my father always flew coach. I'm thinking, they're crazy; they have the money to do this. That will come in time if they travel more. The same with taking the smaller suite rather than the junior suite or the one-bedroom suite. It's a gradual progression that comes with travel and seeing the experiences they might have. With each trip it becomes less about the price and more about the level of comfort.

So they assimilate into becoming comfortable spending money?

What I love about most of my clients is that they were self-made. I find them much more interesting than those who've inherited their wealth and grew up with it their entire life and have their expectations at a certain level. These are people who've really earned their money and they're giving a lot of it away to charity, building beautiful homes, taking care of their families, and spending a lot on cars they might want to drive, trips they might want to take. They're comfortable spending once everything's fallen into place and their business is at a certain level.

Do clients typically come to you with ideas for the hotels and the places they want to go, or are you giving your personal suggestions?

A lot of them do their research. They'll talk to friends, even if they're not at the same income level. If they ask, "we're going to Buenos Aires next month, who's been?" on Facebook, a few friends will say stay at the Four

Seasons, then others will suggest bed and breakfasts that they stayed in years ago. I'll have to step in and say, hey I know you guys, I know you did Four Seasons in Uruguay, it's the right hotel for you.

I had one client who said, "Where should I go? I have seven days and I haven't planned my Christmas trip." Budget's not a problem for him, he just wants a great experience, has a new girlfriend. At that moment, I was sitting out on the back of my compound overlooking the ocean. I snapped a picture and said, "This is the place for you, let me check if there's room," and we did the transaction ten minutes from that moment, sitting right there on a beach.

If I'm somewhere and I know there's somebody who hasn't booked a trip, I'll send a picture and say, "I know they have this suite available." That particular client leaves on the 26th and its $4,200 a night, with private jet from the mainland. It was not about the price.

Talk about some of the interesting, hot experiences today. What are the sorts of things that people care about?

We're always asking what the hotels can offer. It ends up being the same stuff. It's more about the clients' interests. We had a client who was going to Bali over Christmas, and it came down to booking a hotel in an area where they could go to three or four different surf spots. We connected with someone local, an expert who could tell them each morning, "Ok, this is where we're going surfing today, because this is going to be the best conditions."

Everyone seems to love the idea of going out on a private boat for a day. It seems to be a crowd pleaser. Just with their family, some staff, and having a day away from the hotel but with all of the amenities.

They rely on us to know not only the guided tour in Paris, but know that the guide speaks perfect English, is vegetarian, and has three kids so she'll be great with the children. We come up with our own experiences beyond what the hotel feeds to us.

Are they interested in all of the details, or do they just want to know that it's all taken care of?

They do, at the end of it. They want everything in one place in an easy to read format. They don't want to have stuff all over. They want to have a comprehensive itinerary of everything that's been booked. The files we send need to be accessible and visible on smart phones or tablets.

What about charitable tie-ins. Do people care if a hotel group is affiliated with a charitable donation?

There's so much out there, it's a general expectation that the companies will be involved at some point. I've talked to clients who are breast cancer survivors, and it does strike a chord. Anyone at that level is involved in some way or another with charities. Up in Silicon Valley, their kids are young, and they're involved in school systems. I get a lot of requests to help give a hotel room for a night or something for their kids' auctions. I can't always help, but I try, because then they see that I care about them beyond their business.

Do clients ask about helping them with things other than travel and hotels?

They'll ask us, "we have to take a really important celebrity out to dinner, do you know anybody at a great sushi restaurant near the Mandarin." And I'll help them; I'll reach out to the GM of the hotel, even if I'm not helping with anything else in their trip.

What are some surprising requests for trips that you've come across?

I have one guy who owns a family business in New Jersey. Flies private, spends a lot of money. The kids now are at the age where they want to have a say in what they do. The son wants to go duck hunting, and I'm cringing because it's the last thing I know anything about. But, at ILTM (International Luxury Travel Market), I'm going for an appointment and come across a ranch in Wyoming called Brush Creek ranch, it's a five-star hotel, and they arrange duck hunting. So they're going to go next year.

Some of these more rugged guys want to go fishing down in the Caribbean, or will ask where else they can go. It usually needs to be a combination thing where there's something for the wives and their friends as well. They also travel a lot in groups of friends when they do this type of trip.

They all love to eat. They all want reservations at Jiro's sushi restaurant, and they want to go to the 3 a.m. private tour of the fish market before the tourists get there.

What about things like cycling trips, where you're biking in the country side?

Definitely, some people want to cross that off their bucket list.

What about events, like Art Basel, or college football games, or Formula 1?

We always have some Formula 1. Hotels triple rates, seven-night minimum, but people don't care, they just want to go. Same with last minute Super Bowl trips. They wait until last minute. A lot is last minute. We can always find a way to make it happen as long as they're willing to pay. And they are.

Any other things you could talk about specifically to working with this Super Rich people?

We always talk when it comes to luxury travel about having clients greeted upon arrival, and VIP, all to the max…that needs to be toned down with these Super Rich clients, because they don't want to feel uncomfortable. They want to be treated well, but some of my clients prefer privacy. They're not using their real name in certain places, and we need to work with hotels that understand that. Finding out if there are doors in the back where they can get in and out without being seen. It's more important than the style of the room. They want rooms and suites we can book out to have multiple rooms for these clients. They just don't want to be bothered. They don't want to be part of the scene. They're less concerned about going to hotels to see and be seen, or boast to friends.

Have you seen clients change when they've become billionaires and millionaires?

No, a lot of them built their businesses and earned their money. They like being treated well, and they like treating people well. Bill Fischer told me many years ago when I interviewed him that "there are a lot of rich people out there, but we want to work with the nice ones." If clients are not pleasant to deal with, or if they're being an asshole, we don't like to work with them. There are a few that get arrogant, or don't treat my team nicely. I've said to two people in the last few weeks that we're not the right company to deal with their travel.

Have you ever let go of a difficult client?

I had one client who was very nice, and married a woman who wasn't nice to my team, always calling us at 2 a.m. harassing us. Everything was an emergency. It wasn't how we were accustomed to working with him. I'm careful to protect my team. We want to keep filling out the client base with wealthy clients who appreciate what we do for them.

When you're booking people to London and Paris, are they loyal to the hotels they've stayed at, or do they want to try new places?

I'll tell them, I think you'd really like Le Royal Monceau, the new Philippe Starck hotel. The bar's really cool, indoor pool, maybe you'd like to try that. And the next time they'll try the Maurice. They're always open. I'll find out what type of neighborhood they like, and try to match the client with the experience.

It's a myth that they always want hip, trendy, design-focused hotels... some do! Maybe they want to stay at the Ace Hotel in New York on business, or in London they want to stay at the Savoy or the Bristol in Paris, because it's the palace they've heard about. They want five-star service in a boutique environment, and it feels like luxury.

CHAPTER 5

MAN CAVE FOR BILLIONAIRES

Interview with ... Nick Linca
MANAGING PARTNER, PROVIDENT JEWELRY

U nder Nick Linca, Provident Jewelry has established itself as one of America's top sellers of high-end watches, with prices often ranging well into six figures. Among the brands Linca sells are: Arnold & Son, Carl F. Bucherer, Cartier, Chanel, Christophe Claret, Chopard, Louis Moinet, MB&F, Parmigiani and Ulysse Nardin. To sell timepieces regularly that are three times what the average American makes in a year, is just the starting point.

How did you get into the business?

I had a new girlfriend who was going to stick around for a while, and being of the Romanian background, that's where my family is from, I don't like paying retail. So I went Christmas shopping for jewelry, because that's what you do when you first want to impress a girl. I went ahead, and went to The Gardens Mall in Palm Beach Gardens, Florida, and stopped at the first jewelry store that I stumbled upon—Zales Jewelers. I was at the time, 16 years old. They had a sign "help wanted" in the window, so aside from buying a little ring, I also asked for a job, and was hired approximately three weeks after, after being relentless on the phone. They did the background check and I started at $8 an hour as a cashier. They were understaffed, so I started selling, and ended up selling more than some of the top salespeople who had been there for years.

Where did you go from there?

Within eighteen months, I was store manager of Zales in The Gardens Mall. I had just turned 18. I made the Elite Club, which is the most prestigious managerial award, and won a trip to the Cowboys Stadium in Dallas, where they had the Blues Brothers perform. I really liked the business.

My initial run-in with high-end luxury watches was through my father, who passed me down with his Omega, when I was about 17. His best friend, that he had sponsored to come to the United States, was a gentleman that worked at a small jewelry store at The Mall at Short Hills, called Orologio. And, I was wondering why, when they have all of these calculator watches and stuff that I was interested in, does this guy have to buy a watch-winder to put his watch in. It seemed antiquated. Why didn't he just get a quartz watch, it's at least 10,000 times more accurate and 1,000 times less expensive, so why not go for that? He explained the mechanics of it, and how he enjoyed winding it, and giving life to it every morning. I grabbed a bit of that passion.

So fast forward—I'm manager of Zales, I took a store in my region in South Florida from 9th place to 2nd place. So from second to last, to second behind the Zales in Boca Raton. Accolades and kudos. And, all that until we had a mangers meeting and my father was very sick, he had a pancreas and kidney transplant back then. So I couldn't attend the managers meeting due to the fact that he was at the hospital. When the regional manager told me at the time that he suggests that I skip the hospital and make the meeting, that's when I said here's my two weeks' notice.

After Zales, is that where you got into high luxury sales?

At the time, there were two big amazing jewelry stores upstairs that I dreamed of working for. One of which was Mayor's. The other was Hamilton Jewelers. They came by, shopped me, and offered me a position. Working for them coming from Zales, I might as well have been selling Persian rugs. It had nothing to do with what I had known. I couldn't relate to the price points, I couldn't relate to the extravagant clients who would spend on a watch, or a ring, as much as my townhouse is worth, or three or four times that. But one thing stood true—they wanted the personal relationship, they liked conversing with someone with worldly experience. And, I had traveled the world since I was 16 months old, spending the majority of the time with my father. We would lease a car in France; go from France to Germany, to Austria, to Hungary, spend summers in Romania, Transylvania and Bucharest for four months, and he opened my eyes to how privileged I was to have been born in America.

An American's dream is—what can they do, what can they purchase, and what can they buy, versus a Romanian's dream of how can I get to America? They want to work hard for these things, they don't want to win the lottery, or fly a private plane. They just want a fair shot, they want to express their talents and work hard. So, Hamilton Jewelers for ten years, that's when I learned about function versus purpose, and the power of the one percent. I remember those things, and I always wanted to have something of my own.

How did you become a partner in Provident?

It was started by Rob Samuel's father, Art. Art was a Navy Commander; he retired, and had a passion for gems. He opened Provident Jewelry & Loan in West Palm Beach. He's known as a big authority in jade and ivory today. I met Rob after many trips to Basel, and Rob's business plan up until I came on board was based on two locations, one in West Palm Beach, and one in Naples. His main business was high-end jewelry, mainly estate goods, and also some pawn and loan, but only for big transactions.

In West Palm Beach, there were deals that needed to be closed, real estate deals, etc. A guy came in the first time I interviewed, needed a half a million dollars immediately so he could close on a real estate deal until the bank approved. The guy brings in a seventeen carat asscher cut diamond, brings in his collection of Rolexes, and is loaned half a million dollars for a period of thirty days. Then took them back, or sold some. I liked the business plan, the writing was on the wall with the market the way it was, with the inflation, and real estate prices, and the mortgage business, but it couldn't continue to go this way. A small little townhouse that was $50,000 in West Palm Beach could not possibly go to $350,000. I had a feeling but I didn't know that it was going to be that bad.

When Rob offered me a position to talk about opening a higher end store, that wasn't just about pawn and loan and estate goods, and I didn't really have the connections and know-how, and customer service to truly exceed clients' expectations, in that model that I was kind of bred into. But I didn't want to work for someone else, so I put together a business plan that we agreed upon, and we opened a store in Jupiter, which was the first location of its kind. Super high-end. The designer of the stores was Sherif Ayad, world-renowned, and he designs malls and homes around the world, including Dubai and Singapore. He was a friend of Rob's, and put together a gorgeous plan for the Jupiter location. And we started. I became a partner. And, then we took it a step further, instead of just keeping it a regular jewelry store with the same old events, the same old things. I really wanted to create that 'third place,' not home, not work, but Provident.

When you say you wanted Provident to be the 'third place,' you're saying the same thing that Howard Schultz wanted for Starbucks and what Steve Jobs wanted with Apple Stores. Is that where you got it from?

I had the idea, and never read his book, but when I said it later, someone said, oh, that's what Schultz said. But we wanted that, because we weren't in a tourist location, like St. Thomas, St. Croix, with cruise ships parking outside and tourists coming in, and I see them for fifteen minutes and then never again, and trying to show them as much as I can in fifteen minutes.

How has the 'third place' idea worked in practice?

So this 'third place' idea, in 2008, the big bubble burst, and with Madoff, Palm Beach County was affected quite heavily, and luckily, we had enough capital to sustain all of these buys. In 2008, we had two locations, to now where we have six Provident locations. The first was in Clematis Street in downtown West Palm Beach which has been there for 21 years. We plan on opening a hotel, a ten story hotel in West Palm Beach, on the corner of Dixie and Clematis Street as a luxury boutique hotel.

So there's West Palm Beach which is the first location, followed by the second location on Fifth Avenue in Naples. The third being in Jupiter, the fourth location being in Ft. Meyers, the fifth being an additional Naples location, that's five times as large. Then, we just opened up a small shop on Worth Avenue in Palm Beach.

How do you target the Super Rich?

I try not to target or treat anyone different from the next person. It's about the person, about the experience, and we try to offer that experience. That's why we expanded our Jupiter location a year ago to Dream Factory, which is a $600/square foot build-out, and is thirteen hundred square feet. You can come in and have a drink, we have a full bar that can sit comfortably eight people. We have a walk-in smoke room, where clients can enjoy a cigar without offending the eighty-five percent non-smokers. Everything's complementary. Aside from the bar and walk-in humidor, we have forty-two humidified boxes.

How did you transition Provident's image to the Ultra High Net Worth (UHNW) client base you wanted, and what type of marketing did you use?

From transitioning to Hamilton to Provident, initially, and opening up what would be the next generations of jewelers, it was tough, because whenever I mentioned the name Provident, they didn't look at it like Provident Jewelry, the authorized dealer of this, where there's great service. It was oh, Provident Jewelry the pawn shop? It took about four years to fine-tune the staff, hire the best watch-maker, exceed client expectations. About fifteen percent come in from the advertising. I look to further validate who we are with the luxury brands. Sixty percent are from referrals, if not seventy percent. We truly offer the people the experience they look for when buying luxury, and therefore, they feel comfortable referring us to their friends.

Once you get an UHNW client, what makes them keep coming back?

I have a theory, and it's not just mine—everyone has the best doctor, everyone has the best attorney, got the best deal on their car, but paid the most for their house. That's what their deal is. So someone says, I have a great jeweler, well why? Why is it the best jeweler? Well, they fixed this or that. But you paid for it. What else happened? They got it done early, they called to follow-up. It's the service. But I found that husbands didn't really want to go to the jewelry store. Nobody says, oh, honey let's spend our Saturday going jewelry shopping. That never happens. So what we did was we bought the entire strip of our plaza, and rented out two of the five units to a high-end salon spa. We collected our rent in gift-certificates at a discount. We brought a salon and spa into our space. They can go get a complimentary something, and now the husbands can come in and have a smoke, drink some Johnny Blue, watch a game, talk with their friends. The locker system is really cool, because the forty-two humidified lockers that we have we give out to our really good clients. Someone who comes to the four or five annual occasions, or someone who drops a hefty amount of money, around a quarter of a million and up. With that said, we offer those clients, which started in 2015, a locker holder, and four months a year we're going to have a member guest event. We're making ourselves a destination.

My thought was—if someone said to me, hey I just flew into Florida, let's not golf, let's go to my jeweler and have a cigar and a scotch. What does that even mean? Jeweler, cigar, scotch? Well the CEO of this, or the president of that, or the retired person from there, have been coming in on a regular basis. There's one person I'd like to talk about who has a book out, he was the CEO of five separate companies in different industries, to the point where a publishing company came to him and approached him and said, how can you possibly be a manager of home-goods, oil, toys, all of these things. The gentleman comes in once a week, every week. If it's before 11, he'll come in for a cigar and a cappuccino, and if it's after two, he'll come in for a whiskey and a cigar. He was talking about going to Basel with his buddy, and last year he had dinner with the Pope and the Prime Minister of Israel in one week. A real gentleman.

In dealing with the Super Rich, they don't want to be treated like kings or queens, they want to make sure people are listening to them. They don't want you to tell them things twice.

No-brainer. Absolutely. It's about having them come and visit and spend time with you, not selling them something. It's about remembering those dates and hearing what they say.

So you get the referral, who are they talking to right off the bat?

We have our sales staff, which is like our family. We have a lady who has been with us, going on 15 years. We've never had someone leave. We had someone pass away unfortunately from cancer, but everyone's been there from day one.

Someone comes, a billionaire, do you take the lead?

Absolutely not, everyone is there to treat everyone the same. They know the system that we have in the store. Although it's a commission, the commission is not the big portion of the equation. The last thing I want is for someone to sell someone something due to a spiff, due to an incentive. I rarely allow any sort of spiffs and incentives in my store from our brands.

If I'm on the Forbes list, do you call me back or do you have one of your salespeople?

Doesn't make a difference. It depends on what you're asking for. Everyone knows, the sales people know, that I have myself, my business partner Seth Berman, and then I have a gentleman on my staff who's very knowledgeable about watches and timepieces, and cars, and jets.

Do you find that your customers that are coming and buying watches and jewelry for $500,000, are also asking what's a good place to go in the Caribbean?

Absolutely. I have a close friend of mine that I met as a customer initially, he had a small start-up at the time, and five years later made it onto the business list of *Inc.*, so he took a $300,000 investment, and is now turning down $100 million, $120 million for his rehab centers. He's become a close friend. He has two airplanes, a G3 and another. For my birthday we go to Vegas together, we watched Mayweather together. He consistently asks me to start a website called "Ask Nick" because he feels that I have all the answers. He'll call me to get a reservation at such and such restaurant where his Black American Express can't even get him in.

One of the neatest things that someone's ever done for me is that a gentleman who I dealt with from the Hamilton days had forgotten the gift for his wife's 50th anniversary. I opened up The Gardens Mall Hamilton at midnight, had the police, had the security there, I opened up the vault and I picked up something for him, and wrapped it. This is going back nine years ago. Two years ago, he called me and said, you've always been there, whenever I call you, whether it's a strap, a watch, something for my wife, what can I do for you? I said, your friendship and your loyalty is enough. So what he does is that he pays me with his Black American Express. I said, you know what, Arnold, I would like to have one of these one day. I didn't know his best friend was the COO of American Express. He says text me your social security, your name, and your address. I get home after my birthday party and I have Black American Express at my front door, no annual fee, all compliments of him. It's all relationships.

You said before that a lot of the people who came from your wedding were also well-to-do clients. Can you categorize the Super Rich clients, are they different? Are there those who want to buy stuff from you but hey, Nick, I don't need you in my personal life?

I haven't had one of those situations yet.

So with the well-to-do clients, you become part of their life?

I find that, at times, especially at the beginning of the relationship, there are those that because of their wealth try to cross that line of speaking a certain way, or asking something of you that's not normal. Or you call them at a bad time and they're abrupt. At which point, I put an end to the conversation, I say it sounds like you're busy, it sounds like you're a bit aggravated due to something else, why don't you give me a call when you have a moment to talk to me. It generally draws them back a bit and they know that oh, you know what, I'm wrong, and he called me on it. I'll do anything for you. Don't speak to me like some blackjack dealer that gave you three bad hands in a row.

And will you 'fire' these customers?

Absolutely not. To a certain degree. If it comes to being rude, and I catch them on a bad day, and they're being rude, if they continue and come back down to their senses and they realize that you can't tip me a few hundred dollars to tip me away, or pay me to be abused. Every now and then they'll test that water.

In Palm Beach you're in an interesting place. Talk to me about what you're doing with the investment in art shows? Who goes to them?

The Palm Beach shows enable Provident Jewelry to be in all of the major cities in the United States. My partners started The Palm Beach Show Group 11 years ago, which started as a show at the convention center, before it was even the convention center. They decided to bring a true luxury show, not with curtains, but with hard walls, and with some of the best dealers in the world. It's the largest family-owned show in the United States of America. We started 11 years ago with Palm Beach, then we acquired Baltimore, with the Baltimore Spring Antique and Art Show, the number 1 revenue producing show for the city of Baltimore. Then we started Dallas, and experimented with D.C.

Baltimore?

Baltimore! There's a lot of wealth in Baltimore. There was already a show there, but an existing show that had a flawed business plan. We picked it up six years ago, and it's our largest show. Jewelry, arts, and antiques.

Are the Super Rich people that come in as knowledgeable as you would expect, about which watch has the highest retail value, or which diamond really is cut correctly?

Our business has changed tremendously over the last 15 years. Our clients are loaded up with information to the extent that they're becoming a danger to themselves. Everyone believes that the color is—how clear the diamond is, or the clarity is—how much it sparkles. They know the terms, and the pronunciation, but don't really understand them and what they mean. So I like to break it down into this. Why did the GIA start the color at a D and not an A? Because they wanted to be sure that if they found a whiter diamond than an A, they didn't want to confuse the public like the pearl industry did with A, A+, AA, AAA+. So when you speak to a person and you focus on the relationship, you focus on telling them about yourself and themselves, and what they truly want. Do they want the biggest because their friend has the biggest and they have a limited budget? Or do they have an unlimited budget and they want the best and the finest? Asking questions is key. And, explaining as if I was speaking to my mother or my wife. I'm going to guide you the way I'd guide my mother or my wife to buy something.

Once you have a customer, what do you do with CRM (Customer Relationship Management)?

It's remembering important dates. So for example, here in my bag, I have something for my close friend, she inherited about $800 million from her late husband. Been married for 20 years. She's golfed over 2,200 golf courses and 99 countries. She has a lot of class and a lot of stories. I know she likes marzipan, so I stopped at a chocolate store and got her marzipan and pistachio chocolate bars.

How do you keep track of it all?

We keep it in our database, and also in our mind. If a client is celebrating an event, we put it into the database, send them a wine at the restaurant where they're celebrating, or have a bakery deliver to that restaurant.

If an anniversary is coming up, do you reach out?

We reach out constantly, not just because of an anniversary. We're reaching out just because.

How do you communicate?

We let them choose—do they do better with text, or email. All my employees have their own phones, they text from their own phones, not worried about taking the phones when they leave and taking those clients. I'm part of the transaction. While they're shopping for jewelry, I bring them a mimosa or glass of champagne, I offer a cigar and talk sports. They become part of the Provident Jewelry family, not just the salesperson's personal friend, but everyone's friend. Everyone knows everyone's name; you greet that client just as if they were walking into your home.

You see the big brands becoming sponsors of major events. Does that translate into selling your customers?

Last year we supported 56 charities, everything from the LLS to Furry Friends, to the Big Dog Ranch Rescue, to the American Heart Association, to the local schools, to the Benjamin School. Because we like to give, and because when we built the Dream Factory, we had one thing in mind—we're going to do as many charities as possible, to give the store up to friends of Provident. So next month, we have a client and friend, Herb, who started a dog shelter rescue, and is having an event. He brings his invite list of 150-200 people, and last year we gave a 1k diamond to put into a champagne glass with some CZ's, and people were buying glasses for $100 or $200, and someone ended up with the diamond. These people come to our store for the event, some haven't been there before. They bring in the bartenders, etc.

Beyond the bigger brands, how important is it that they've already heard about a product?

It certainly helps sometimes. Some brand conscious people really just want the Rolex or Cartier, and other people aren't buying for someone else, but really for themselves.

So the fact that they're not really that aware of the niche brands isn't important for you?

Not that important to me. I believe in the brands. I don't just pick up a brand that's here today, gone tomorrow.

CHAPTER 6

DO THE UHNWS CARE ABOUT BRANDS?

Interview with ... Henry Kim
EXECUTIVE VICE PRESIDENT OF SALES,
WHEELS UP

A closed sale by Henry Kim has ranged upwards of $10 million. While his new post as Executive Vice President of Sales for start-up Wheels Up democratizes private aviation travel starting at about $4,000 per hour, in his career selling fractional shares of private jets for Flexjet and NetJets his customers paid multiple millions of dollars to start, followed by monthly management fees in the tens of thousands of dollars, and then hourly rates to fly, plus catering and other fees. Typical customers were often worth over $50 million.

Talk about where you're getting your leads and prospects. Are they from corporate marketing programs, or are you developing them yourself?

There are so many different angles that we utilize from a marketing and PR standpoint for us to generate leads. I've been in the private aviation sector for almost 11 years now. I've got a pretty diverse knowledge base regarding how the private aviation consumer goes about their decision-making process. From a marketing standpoint, the publications that make the most sense for our vertical are: Wall Street Journal, Forbes, Fortune magazine. Unique partnerships and events are also important lead generators that also deliver great buzz and PR.

So those leads for you that come down the pipeline, do you and your associates follow up on them?

Absolutely! Something that also creates immediate buzz would be when Kenny Dichter, CEO and Founder of Wheels Up goes on CNBC or Squawk Box. We see a direct correlation to the phones ringing and the website traffic and inquires. When he went on with the CEO of Textron Aviation, it generated so much call volume that the website almost crashed because of the volume of website traffic. Those are instant pops from a marketing and lead gen perspective.

So much in the private aviation space is also contingent on word of mouth and member referrals. You have to establish credibility or trust in the market space in order to have any sustainability. Our members are people that are in the know—and there's only a degree of separation between those who travel privately—they know who the providers are. When you consider the tri-state area—it's such a mature market as it relates to private aviation and, when it relates to options and choices, people learn quickly who the newcomers are, what their business model is, what their sweet spot is. It's also about attracting the right type of influencers who see the value, which creates a wildfire effect. They tell a friend, that person tells a friend, and the momentum builds upon itself.

Is branding important in the private aviation space?

One of the reasons I chose to come to Wheels Up was based upon who was at the helm. Kenny Dichter and Bill Allard. Some of the guys who've been in the space for a while that truly understand the value of branding and marketing. Kenny is one of the pioneers in private aviation branding. He's a master. So I have no doubt that Wheels Up will be one of the most recognized private aviation brands within the next two to three years. We're already seeing it.

Most of my tenure was at Flexjet, and then I went to NetJets. Then the opportunity with Wheels Up came through. It was an educated, low risk move that's paying off in massive dividends.

Would you find that the prospects you're talking to know the brand already?

Most of the real potential buyers are very well educated and well versed in who the key providers are. With us being the new entrants, we needed to do some educating, but we had a very familiar and compelling story to tell. It was then about providing them with a solution that fit their personal needs.

Were they really familiar with the details of what each of the various private aviation companies offered?

They had a basic understanding of who the players were but were not familiar with the nuances and details of what the key differentiators were. That's the Sales Executive's role, to provide them with that education and walk them through that consultative sales process.

So you talk to someone who is well off, they've probably flown private before, what was something that they didn't know that surprised you?

Most of them were pretty well educated. They understand that there are certain things that are standard in the industry. Like billing—most private aviation providers bill for actual flight time plus taxi and landing time. But people made assumptions based on crew duty. They make the assumption that if you fly privately, you could call for an aircraft in a 24 to 12-hour window depending on the size of your aircraft that you bought (access via a fractional or jet card program). They thought that it was at your disposal wherever and whenever, irrespective of whether it exceeding a crew's ability to fly within FAA legal parameters.

So you get a lead, what is the company giving you in regards to background, or is it up to you to research before that initial contact?

We have a great sales operations set-up, that does a tremendous job of vetting our leads. If an incoming lead comes in, we'll do some basic due diligence to establish some history and commonality in the potential customer. We have a CRM (Customer Relationship Management) solution that we use, and when we get a lead our sales operations team will fill in the fields in our CRM solution that give a bio on who our particular lead is. If they can find it online—even from a basic Google search—where he might be traveling to, what boards he sits on, what type of philanthropic work they're involved in.

So someone's called in, requested information, the lead management team has put together the bio. What comes next?

We have a word that's part of our philosophy called "suddenness"—which is reacting at a very fast pace, because it's a fast-changing marketplace. The benefit of being first is huge, while we have the prospects mindshare. So attacking that opportunity via phone, followed up by an email is crucial. Ideally, you want to have an initial phone conversation so that you can establish some rapport and conduct a needs analysis.

Do you find that when someone comes to you they're also requesting information from other providers?

Usually, yes. They're either with a provider and having some sort of service issue or are coming to term with their contract, and looking for either a more efficient or better solution to fit their needs.

What's the gist of the initial conversation?

The initial conversation is about understanding the prospects needs and uncovering the who, where, when, and how. Who they're currently using, where are they typically traveling, when are they traveling, how often are they going. When you get those basic questions answered, you have a pretty good picture of their needs and whether or not we would be a good fit for them. Just because they have the ability and financial means to fly privately, does not mean that we will be a perfect solution for them and its incumbent upon the Sales Exec. to walk them through the consultative process to ensure they understand our value proposition.

Are you dealing with the principal, the gatekeeper or a combination?

It's 80-20. 80 percent of the time you're dealing with the principal, because especially for Wheels Up—our entry point is so low, it is only $17,500 to join—a lot are using our solutions for personal travel. So because it's personal for them and their family, they want to make the decisions on their own, they want to make decisions personally. We're typically dealing with the end user or principal.

Our membership model can also be integrated into an existing solution they already have in play, whether they have a whole aircraft, a fractional interest, or if they have a jet card. The market has become so mature, so savvy, that the members often times already have a solution in play and they can just integrate our service into their pre-existing portfolio.

So maybe you're a C-level executive at IBM, you spend most of your flights on IBM corporate jets, and you don't want to go back to commercial for your leisure?

We work with flight departments as well and have been able to seamlessly integrate our membership model as a great supplemental solution for a corporate flight department. Our fleet of King Air 350i's allows us to do the heavy lifting for a lot of their simple, regional trips without having to put a lot of wear on their heavy metal. It essentially provides corporate flight departments with a cost effective multiple use option to supplement their existing needs.

What's your typical ongoing interaction with them?

We maintain a quarterly touch-point at minimum. But we obviously base it upon the customer. Some folks are very private in nature, they want to be touched when they want to be touched, and others are very hands on. It's about knowing your customer at the end of the day, what their personality type is. You try to come up with a schedule that systematically addresses their needs, and come up with a way for them to give feedback, so we can make adjustments. Some of them were like—Henry, I'm fine, I'll contact you, don't contact me. And others want to be very engaged, they want to come to our events, they want to help build what we're growing.

What sorts of events are you guys doing?

That's one of the great things about our model. Our primary goal is Wheels Up, but there's also an integral Wheels Down component of our business, the lifestyle, experiential events that we host. Some of the key ones that we do revolve around Art Basel, The Super Bowl and The Masters down at Augusta. We'll have a hospitality venue at most of the key national sporting events as well.

Speaking back to your experience at Flexjet and NetJets, what were some of the events that were most successful? Anything that surprised you?

We'll dabble and try different venues, but the core is the three I just mentioned. In addition, we'll throw in additional regional events. And the regional managers and the sales executives can dictate what demographic they're trying to attract. In the South, in Texas for example, we're trying to incorporate hunting. The hunting vertical in general is a very attractive, event-oriented experience in the Southern region. In the West Coast, we had a partnership with the Napa Valley Film Festival. In the East, it's a combination of everything. Northeast is still a finance driven vertical in the private aviation sector. So we're looking at events compelling for that market—and it tends to be sporting events. Sports are one of our lowest common denominators that attracts the maximum interest. We have partnered with USA Basketball at Madison Square Garden. We gave great tickets to members and prospects to attend. We did a great Q&A session with (Coach) Jim Boeheim of Syracuse, and had some NBA players come do a meet-and-greet with our customers and take some pictures. We also host a Post-Heisman Brunch for our members after the Heisman and will have some of our Ambassadors like Kirk Herbstreit conduct a Q&A with former Heisman recipients. It's all about the delivering a unique and memorable experience for our members and delivering maximum value.

Any other events like that that have been very successful?

Golf is very big for us as well. It always has been. We have testimonial after testimonial from professional PGA golfers using private aviation to extend the longevity of their playing career. It allows them to leave at a moment's notice if they want to go to a venue. It increases their quality of life and their longevity on tour. We're tapping into that as well and have some tremendous Ambassadors such as Ricky Fowler and Nick Faldo.

Besides the major sports, the horse vertical is also very good and obviously hit a grand slam with American Pharaoh. I have also been a part of The Hampton Classic, Bridgehampton Polo and Greenwich Polo. We try to cover as many target rich verticals in the sporting arena as possible.

What about the importance of family when it comes to events?

That is huge and most of our events are family centric. As a father I can speak to this as well. If your kids enjoy something, the parents will go out of their way to make it to a particular event or venue. So, for example, private concerts—the Miley Cyrus concert. One of the members raved to me after a Miley Cyrus concert, saying that he was now untouchable in the house and could walk on water—he lived with his wife and three daughters. Two daughters attended the concert with him, and the girls became the most popular kids at school. She attributed this to the father getting the tickets. He said, "I'm the hero in the household." We do events not only for the parents, but for their children. As the adage goes: "a parent is only as happy as their unhappiest child." So we know that if we can make a child happy, we can make the parent happy. We correlate that experience with our branding.

What events are good for prospecting?

I would say that the sporting events and concerts have the greatest ROI. You have to understand something. Events are a double-edged sword. It's a way to reward the member with an experience so that they can link that experience with the brand that delivered it for them. If you do that, they'll bring other folks who are interested in learning about the provider. It's the hidden gem. It's meant to be a defensive weapon—to keep customers—but it's also a way to create good will that will encourage them to share us with friends.

What about third party events that you've attended? Financial conferences, boat shows, and so on?

I would say that I've been to about 100 plus events in my time. In the New York area, you could attend a high-end luxury event every day of the week here in the city. It's about picking and choosing. To go into the mindset that you're going to close this amount of business as a result of attending this event, it's just not going to happen. It's about creating as many touch-points, in order to build brand awareness. The people you typically meet at third party events are great relationship builders, great influencers that can attract you to the end user at the end of the day. It also establishes yourself as a credible resource in the marketplace.

Also, at football games, some of the pre and post tailgates are absolutely exorbitant in nature. They'll have chandeliers in tents, and high-end caterers and chefs prepare the barbeque for the tailgate. They'll be dressed to the nines, especially down south in SEC country. They spare no expense for hospitality. It's a high-end luxury event. It blew my mind, as it relates to what you expect a tailgate to be.

Do you find many customers attending college football, NASCAR, things you might not associate as 'luxury events?'

Absolutely! When big football games are played, our flight volumes always increase. Football alumni travel well and are extremely loyal with regard to supporting their schools both figuratively and financially.

Are there any other surprising drivers for private jet usage?

Another key vertical is the family pet—I can't tell you how many decisions have been made based on the family dog. The idea of their beloved dog or animal being stuck in a commercial airline storage area is not an option for these people. So they'll make the decision based on the family dog. It's amazing how many deals I've closed because of the dog.

The dog is a vital component of the family decision process. When they join a program, we'll provide a gourmet gift basket for the pet, an embroidered collar with their name, membership cards in the dog's name instead of the owner's name. We'll make gourmet, gluten-free dog-treats if we know that the dog is an integral part of the decision making process. You cannot underestimate the importance of the family pet. Most people overlook it, but it's very important. They'll come out and ask you, can I bring my pet on board? When you tell them that they can keep their pet in the cabin with you, it always brings a huge smile to their face.

Do you find that clients come to you and ask you for advice with other things?

Yes, that's true, and that's why we have so many unique partnerships with other high-end luxury service providers and manufacturers. It goes hand-in-hand. We try to align ourselves with the appropriate providers. We want to ensure that our brands are aligned from a cultural, sales, and execution standpoint. We'll use our partnerships to ensure that we can provide our customers with whatever they need.

Do you get people coming to you and saying, "Henry, you must know good hotels in London?" or "I'm trying to find this Patek watch?"

Not that often, but we know that our members appreciate a concierge type of service. That's why we have a member service team available 24 hours a day, 365 days a year. A certain limo, or SUV, or helicopter, or hotel accommodations. We also have a unique partnership with a high end concierge service that all our members have access to for dinner reservations, show tickets, sporting events, etc.

What about contact? Do you send newsletters, communications? What sort of information are they interested in hearing from you?

We send a quarterly newsletter. They want to know how we're doing, where our services are expanding, and events they might be interested in. It keeps them abreast of what's going on, because we're obviously growing at a very rapid pace. So our quarterly newsletter is something that our members read. And if we are attending an event where we'll announce an expansion, we'll also keep our readers and owners updated.

What type of net worth are you dealing with? Where do they make their money?

I would say that to the layperson, the assumption is that we're dealing with superstars, celebrities, Hollywood actors. That's not the normal case. 90% of our membership base, over the ten plus years I've been in the industry, are self-made people who grew up with middle-class values, but wound up having a tremendous amount of personal and financial success which affords them the ability to fly private. From a demographic perspective, and we did some studies on it, most people have an excess of $20 million net worth. You have to have a certain liquid spend as it relates to travel requirements. In this sector—and I've always covered the New York region—it's heavily finance focused. Investment banks, hedge funds, private equity. They look at it from a time-value of money perspective. So they can quantify the productivity that private aviation affords them. Private aviation is more justifiable for that vertical.

If you talk nationally, where do you see some of the customers coming from?

Most of private aviation emanates from the "smile states." If you go out of the northeast to the Midwest, you still have a heavy financial focus, with Chicago as an epicenter for finance. But you also have people that have multiple businesses in multiple locations around the Midwest, and need private aviation to visit multiple factories in one day. To them, it's about efficiency.

And what type of industries are these factories?

Everything from manufacturing to alpaca farms who provide the fleece for Patagonia jackets. We have customers in the Midwest who are chicken farmers who sell to the larger OEM manufacturers. The food industry is big in the Midwest. Down south you have tourism, leisure-driven wealth. The Florida market is a degree separated from the New York market, so it's very much leisure driven. Dallas is energy and oil, a huge corridor that continues to be extremely successful. In southern California, you have more of the entertainment community. Then up north you have the technology sector, VC firms, IT companies. Aspen and Colorado are big destinations. During the winters for skiing, and during the summer for other outdoors experiences.

Do you see the same level of interest in luxury goods from self-made wealth or unconventional wealth?

Definitely! Whether it's the food industry, or the dental industry, people make assumptions about how financially viable it will be in the long-term, but you couldn't be further from the truth. These people have a sustainable business model that generates significant profits for them to fly privately. They may come from these under the radar industries but they are wearing expensive watches, buying expensive jewelry, staying in expensive hotels and buying expensive designer clothing.

What about charitable tie-ins, are those things important to your clients?

Absolutely. That's a huge component. Most of our members belong to at least one or multiple boards for charitable or philanthropic causes. They see our branding. They see our awareness. We evaluate from the corporate vigilance stance—to do the right thing—but also see if we can make it a win-win by targeting the right audience. Whether it's donating hours to the Make-A-Wish Foundation or the Alzheimer's Drug Discovery Foundation, if there's an opportunity for us to gain exposure on people who are on the board, we'll look at those partnerships and see if we can make a "win win" out of it.

We find that it fits both needs. We're doing good from a corporate standpoint, building the brand, and also making it a prospecting opportunity to those who have a high propensity to become members.

Making the sale, what's the influence of the spouse, gatekeepers and so on?

I would say that the one thing that you can never lose sight of, is that people want to see what they're purchasing. They want to have a test flight or a static viewing of the aircraft. The huge component in the sales process is the spouse. Women, from a safety perspective, place a significant amount of weight towards it. Call it the mother hen scenario, but they need to have the peace of mind that we have the safety parameters in a row. The wife also helps me upsell. The wife will get on the smaller aircraft then we'll show the mid-size, and the wife will typically lean towards the larger option.

Do you find that you end up socializing with some of your clients?

I would say that 20-25% of the time, you wind up having a personal relationship with them. With private aviation, you have to establish trust. You have to establish your credibility in the space. Everyone's going to do their due diligence. Some of it winds up being a longer term relationship—I get invited to weddings, bar mitzvahs, birthdays, because you get ingrained in their lifestyle. Then you see them at other touch points, and it becomes a long-term relationship. It's one of the things that I love about the business.

Do clients ever ask you about doing business ventures with them?

The ask has been there, I've probably been asked ten to fifteen different times about job opportunities as a result of developing their trust over the years. At the end of the day, I'm passionate about the private aviation sector, and I couldn't be happier with the vertical that I'm in, so I never saw the need to go elsewhere.

Any difference between self-made wealth and inherited wealth in dealing with your clients, or age?

That's where knowing your client really comes in. Knowing who you're dealing with. With an older demographic of a family, 50 or 60 plus, it's about the little things. Keeping pace with their tonality, how they like to communicate, being very thorough, going at their pace. With self-made vs. inherited, it's hard to make generalizations. My friends who aren't in the luxury space will often make assumptions like you must be dealing with demanding rich folks who want what they want, and are mean and nasty. That couldn't be further from the truth. Most of these people, whether they have inherited wealth or not, are wonderful people who you'd never know had this sort of wealth. They don't come off with a sense of entitlement. They understand what you can and can't do, and they appreciate what we do for them. Most people we deal with, though, are self-made, and have the ability to relate to their prior work experiences and upbringing. They understand it. From that perspective, most of our clients are a joy to work with.

What about price, are clients looking for better deals?

It depends on when. Up to 2007, price was never an obstacle. They just said, I'll take what my buddy has. There was no discussion about price. They simply paid for it. Post-2008, the marketplace has changed. They're looking for greater value. They're concerned about the way it looks to fly private, and also concerned about being sensible. I have a line from one customer: "Henry, I'm very blessed to be financially successful to be where I am, to fly private. At the end of the day, whether it's $4,000 or $8,000, it's all stupid. Your solution is just less stupid." So at the end of the day, he understands it. He's well grounded, he sees that it's a luxury to fly private. But he wants to see value. He's going to Nantucket, and knows that he doesn't need a mid-sized plane for his wife and him on a 45-minute flight. So we'll set him up with a King Air, reducing his costs in half and getting him where he needs to go. The marketplace has gotten savvier, and people are making that decision to be wiser with their discretionary spend.

Are your clients using social media, are they using Facebook, Twitter? Do you use that as a way to keep in touch with them?

Yes, absolutely. We're using it as a tool for marketing to our existing customers. They can follow us on Twitter, or like us on Facebook. If they want to contact me, I use LinkedIn, which is probably my most popular social medium because it's more of a professional network. So I'll connect with customers to stay in touch. But we use social media to create a buzz and have visualizations of what we're doing there.

Last week we had an event at Jay Z's 40/40 Club in the city, hosted by Kirk Herbstreit. It was post-Heisman (award ceremony), so he came with (ESPN Game Day colleague) Chris Fowler and did a Q&A for our members and prospects. It was meant to be intimate, more exclusive touch point. We probably had about 120 there. It was intended to be a very high touch-point, family affair. Kids showed up in jerseys, we had guest appearances from Tim Tebow. It was enjoyable and meaningful. We'll put that on social media and people can see what we're doing.

I don't use social media like Facebook to contact clients. Most clients share the idea that they fly private because they like their privacy. So that's why we use LinkedIn because it's more professional.

It's something that we do to attract other audiences, but it's something that we use conservatively in our approach.

A lot of luxury brands are comfortable sponsoring Art Basel Miami. I know Wheels Up sponsors some college football games. Are brands missing a beat with their customers in not pursuing events that seem not on brand, considering how successful Hublot has been with the World Cup and Formula 1?

If you look at the loyalty associated with certain schools, especially with football, being able to utilize our business model, where we're incorporating a ride-sharing ability—for certain loyal alumni of a school to be able to go to a football game at night and be back home in the evening with alumni of their school, is a tremendous ask. So many of our customers will use their membership to go to football games. Which, from a private standpoint, is a very seamless program. We'll see a direct correspondence to where our lift increases to the seasons of certain teams. The same goes for the golfing vertical.

Do you your rich customers taking rental opportunities to heart beyond private jets, with rental jewelry or cars?

After 2008, the ownership model morphed into a leasing model. That occurred because people didn't want to make that large up-front capital commitment and didn't want the depreciation risk. I definitely see the rental model more these days. Purses—you can now rent the latest Louis Vuitton or high end watches with Eleven James. It's about having that accessibility. On the flipside, it creates a unique dynamic from a sales perspective. People are leery with sharing information that they're renting with people, they don't want to let other people know that they're leasing instead of owning. It doesn't generate as many referrals like other aspects of the industry.

You can't make assumptions based on the Super Wealthy based on what car they're driving or what they're wearing. We have so many people pulling up to a private aircraft, not in a Lamborghini or a Ferrari (even though they own them), but it's a Chevy Tahoe or Suburban. I'm having more and more meetings with guys who are in their t-shirt. You need to have an open-minded approach to the sales process and have to do a little more due diligence these days when qualifying prospects.

CHAPTER 7

Using A Board to Create UHNW Business

Interview with … Deborah Calmeyer
CEO and Founder, ROAR AFRICA

R OAR AFRICA is a niche travel company started by Deborah Calmeyer, focused on designing and delivering luxury travel journeys to her native southern Africa. Catering to an Ultra High Net Worth audience for a niche destination presents the dual challenge of constantly generating a pipeline of new customers while leveraging relationships with past customers who are not likely to buy on a regular basis. We talked to Deborah Calmeyer about some of her unique strategies that have proven successful.

Tell us about your background?

I grew up in Zimbabwe, and that's where my love for Africa was born. After the war of liberation my father did not want security and alarms so we got a pet lioness who lived alongside our two Labradors in the house with us. I was the oldest of the four children and got to watch how this animal was so similar to us as human. Forming affectionate bonds with each of us. I formed a close personal relationship with her. That's where my love and appreciation for wildlife was born. After studying further in South Africa and working in Johannesburg, I moved to New York.

Where did you get the idea to start ROAR AFRICA?

Having lived in New York for 16 years now, I've heard many stories of where people have been on safari and how much they loved it. The great thing about Africa is it's so different that everyone loves it. The problem is most people only go once and so they believe the trip they went on was the best, best, best. Usually their trip is planned by someone who is not from there, maybe they have never even been there. The stories of delight that people would tell me of their travels to Africa often led me to force a smile, when inside my heart was sinking. I was thinking "oh no, what a waste, how could anyone have sent you there, charged you that." It became glaringly obvious that the uninformed traveler to Africa was relying on a poorly informed agent. Certainly not a local who planned their trip.

My philosophy whenever I travel is always, always, have someone who is from there plan your trip. The difference is night and day. Otherwise you are getting the easiest trip for your travel agent to sell you. She/he may have been there, but that's a fraction of what it's all about. There are layers and layers to places and getting to the people who are part of the fabric is what will lead you to truly experience it. At ROAR AFRICA I am able to share Africa with people, the way I know it and love it.

There are lots of well-known luxury tour operators featuring Africa. How is what you are doing different?

There are many, yes. It's a great product to sell and when consumers don't have much experience they are none the wiser as to who they are dealing with. My family were Hugenots who arrived in South Africa in 1688 from France. You can see the family tree in the Franschhoek Museum. The family tree begins Daniel Hugo. I am 11th generation South African, so ROAR AFRICA is founded on heritage and passion, we are part of the original core. This is evident by the knowledge, access and resources our guests are privy to. I think there are people that value price, and there are people that value the intimate experience. The intimate experience is for a more sophisticated traveller. I don't think any other luxury provider could arrange for a guest to umpire a national cricket game and have dinner with the team.

What are people spending on the trips you do?

It depends on the type of trip. Sometimes it's a couple, a honeymoon, a family or a small group. I've had a family spend $1 million on a trip, and I have had a honeymoon couple spend $20,000.

Don't many of your clients already have their own private jets?

Yes, many do, but it doesn't always make sense to fly a G5 into South Africa. One generally needs to charter a Pilatus or Cessna Caravan to land on gravel runways in the bush.

When did you actually launch?

In late 2005. This is our tenth year and we are celebrating this milestone with our clients, partners and teams all across the country. Luxury brand Burberry, will be co-hosting events with us to mark this occasion.

So part of the way you got clients when you started the company, you came up with an advisory board?

I've made loads of mistakes as all entrepreneurs do. Burnt my fingers with PR companies, media trips and social media companies. Despite all those trials and tribulations, I have a flourishing business largely due to the incredible network I have cultivated and ROAR AFRICA's exemplary advisory board.

Regarding the advisory board, how did you go and pitch them, and convince them that they should help you out?

My board is made up of people with a passion for Africa. They have all been moved by it in some way. They also understand that tourism is the only industry that can solve Africa's unemployment problem, and that bringing more guests to Africa goes a very long way in creating employment, as well as protecting our wildlife.

Do you end up converting people who say, "I will never go to Africa?" Or do you focus on certain things to look for that might indicate someone being a better prospect?

It's a very sensitive, intuitive read. The value proposition is hard to communicate. Africa changes people, it helps them view the world differently and they are able to reconnect with themselves. I have seen it happen to CEO's, people who've fought in American wars, women and children. We all come away with more and find things we did not know we were looking for. I can tell by the type of guests I am working with before the trip who will really connect with the magic of Africa and be back and who will tick the box.

You mentioned you were talking with the richest man in Ireland, you said you get business through referrals. So when people come to you as referrals, some names you may just know, but I'm sure there are some people that come to you that you just don't know. Are there some procedures you go through to research them, who they are, before you go on the phone?

I always try to Google them. Identify what boards they sit on, charities they support, see what they are passionate about so I can try to include the African version of that.

Do you use social media as a marketing tool?

Yes, we do. I am not sure our key clients use social media much, but I don't think one cannot use social media.

So if you sense that there isn't the right chemistry, you'll tell them you don't want them as a customer?

Yes, I will tell them that we may not be the best fit for them. Bad energy has a domino effect when traveling. If you fight everything in life, then travel will bring out the worst in you. I don't keep any bad energy people near me or on my team. We are a great team, providing the very best service in the industry. We are proactive, gracious and extremely accommodating, but we don't take on horrible people who will mess with our formula. It's not only about making our customers happy, but everyone we touch. Our hotel relationships, our guides, our specialists in wine, food, whatever it is. I have hand-picked the people that make up the ROAR AFRICA experience and none of them deserve to have to endure entitled bad mannered guests. We just don't do bad manners.

Aren't you leaving a lot of cash on the table?

Some people might look at it like that. But that's not the big picture. These kinds of people can destroy the morale of your company. Relationships get tested. A lot of people I work with on the ground in Africa, I know from when I grew up, we went to University together, we share family friends. So when our clients go there, they don't go as number 500 from Company X, they go as Deb's friends from ROAR AFRICA. It's a much more personal thing. And I work hard for it. I go to these properties all the time, I know the chefs, I know the rangers, I know the trackers, I know the owners, I know all of the people in the reservation offices. I know where the sun sets and rises, which room has the best view and the best light. It's why I live between the two countries. These are the relationships that matter in the long term. They are worth the investment, rather than some quick trip that will cause havoc.

It sounds like part of your assets are those relationships with your suppliers?

Absolutely, they are unique friendships built over years. To be treasured and protected.

If you look at generic travel research, it indicates that generally the woman is the driver in travel decisions, but you're now the third person who's told me that it could be the man or the woman, but really it's the HNW individual, the breadwinner, that tends to–go for the high end—control the travel decisions?

I deal with both men and women. I would say probably more men. They are great to work with for the most part, quick decision makers and very appreciative of efficiency. CEO's are usually the most gracious and really delightful to deal with. Perhaps it's because they don't have anything to prove and aren't after a fight. Some people are just not used to doing anything without a fight. It's sad.

Do you find working through assistants can provide challenges?

I like to meet our clients face to face. It's not always possible, but the level we are catering to requires direct contact. Usually that is not an issue unless it's a celebrity, then most likely you will work with the assistant until the guest is actually on the trip.

What would be an example of where you have to translate things?

Having lived in NYC for 16 years I have an acute appreciation for how hard Americans work. How little vacation they take, and therefore how valuable their time is. Helping Africans understand how important time is and how a tiny delay can impact so much for a traveler, and often its someone's only time to do something.

Do you go with a lot of your trips?

I have an entire operation on the ground in Africa. So there is no need for me to go on every trip. Our guests are in ROAR AFRICA's hands all the way.

Are you keeping track as these people are there daily?

Yes, our ground operations team has a figure on the pulse all the time—minute by minute preempting things before a client is even aware of them.

So you're constantly in touch with your service people to make sure your people are happy?

Yes, all the time. I like to know where each guest is, what the weather's like, what they are enjoying. Where they are? Who is doing their massage? What they ate?? What wines on the table? Just things I'll pick up. If they didn't have time for coffee before leaving for their flight to safari— having an espresso on the runway when they land.

One of the interesting things is that generally most of these rich people have made their money doing things like supplying ribs, and so on. We call them "driveway celebrities" because the only time they're famous is when they're at home surrounded by everyone who knows them. It's funny because you'd go to a yacht show and actually meet these people, they would all talk about the fact that they saw the suite in Elite Traveler magazine, and they loved it because they could tell everyone that they slept in the same bed as some celebrity. And things like that. Do you find that having this celebrity is important to the rich people?

One thing I've learned about the culture in America is that celebrities are very important. We have had several on trips, all extremely nice and humble. Of course, our proudest moment was bringing the man who symbolizes Africa in our dreams, back to Africa for the first time since he shot the movie "Out of Africa." It was his first safari, and he absolutely loved his trip with us. He asked if we could arrange all his travel, as he never knew he could travel like that!

What about on price? Obviously these are all very successful business people, but does price ever come up? If so, how do you hold your ground on price?

It doesn't come up much at this level. Especially, if it's a word of mouth referral. Everyone is looking for a deal, but this level of traveler is looking for an experience. Those are the people we deal with.

Do you ask for a budget?

Yes, we try to.

Would you say that most of the trips involve children?

Not little children, because kids under five can't really go on safari. But you know, a lot of trips are for that last family trip before the eldest goes to college, or gets married, or one is living in New York, the other is at college. Multi-generational travel. Or grandpa's been on a few safaris and wants to take the grandchildren and the parents. And, those are my favorite trips because we can do everything privately, we can take the entire lodge, we can cater everything to them, we don't have to cater to other guests, and if they want to stay out there watching the lion eat the buffalo for five hours, great. With the other guests it's always a bit of a balancing act.

When I'm talking to people who sell watches or jewelry or fashion, people are looking for repeat customers. Being so specialized, what percentage of your customers come back?

Probably about 20% are repeat. Many have done up to twelve trips. Some do a trip each year. Africa started off for them as once in a lifetime, so they'll spend more.

Do you have formalized types of post-trip marketing and communications to get them to repeat?

Maybe first it was a couple, and then they want to do a multi-gen trip.

We've had people come for their honeymoon, and then come with their children later. We do reach out all the time to our clients with special events. For example, this year we are celebrating our 10-year anniversary with Burberry who we will do a series of parties across the country with us.

Do you do anything proactively like reaching out to them, calling them?

Yes, we do a lot of very unique events, and I also am a guest speaker quite often on conservation and eco-tourism issues.

You mentioned philanthropy. Is that something that works?

It does sometimes. It depends on what it is. Donating trips for auction doesn't work well. It's a huge amount of work for us to put together, and the people who usually buys these are looking for a deal.

So obviously you talked about San Francisco and Palm Beach. Being a boutique company you have to be targeted. You've got customers from all over the country?

Palm Beach, a lot of New York, Boston, Toronto, Bermuda, San Francisco.

Certain people need to be with a group to be comfortable, very risk-averse, no?

The kinds of guests we work with are trying to escape people. The last thing they want is a group.

You mentioned that the Super Rich are all ADD. But when it comes down to the details do you feel that they are viewing it intently?

Sometimes they haven't even read the itinerary. They'll be on the plane to South Africa with ten guests and I'll start getting texts: "What about this? What about that? Did you organize this?"

It's why I have a huge staff on the ground, why I'm not depending on a ground operator. Because if I had, I would have to relay all that information. Instead, I've already been with the client, I've had dinner with their family. I try to socialize with them, try to invite them to events that we do, try and bring them into the fold, to get to know us, and also for us to know them. I pick up on all sorts of sensitivities, whether it's what kind of wine they had at dinner with me in NY, making sure that that's there for them.

When you're communicating itineraries and details, is it usually by paper or email?

Email and our APP.

How would you quantify the knowledge of these people in terms of their knowledge of international travel, far-off destinations? I mean the perception of these people is that they were extremely knowledgeable and cultured...

American's are knowledgeable about many things, and common destinations like Italy and France. One thing I can do is being an African in America is provide a bridge of confidence. I understand their world and am so thrilled to show them Africa the way that I know it and love it. The truth is that they don't know about Africa, and it can be very overwhelming trying to figure out where to go, who to have help you arrange it.

So what you're doing is educating them politely, not making them feel apprehensive because of their lack of knowledge?

Ensuring that they are confident that they are in the right hands. That everything will be taken care of, and they will not have to think from the moment they touch the ground. And, that I think is what is so incredible for our guides. They love Americans, because they're so hungry for the knowledge. And they are also so generous.

What about shark diving cage, and stuff like that?

There's a large appetite for adventure. They want pictures and stories. It's all about creating those amazing stories to share.

Any other things you would talk about, or discuss, in dealing directly with these people. Your clients run the gamut. Are the Super Rich people different from the run of the mill affluent people?

Each trip is different and designed from scratch to cater to the needs of each individual. What the Super can't buy is time. So its value is enormous, and our job is to maximize it in whatever shape or form.

What do you look for when you're hiring your guides?

How fast they walk. I say that because how fast someone walks will tell you how fast they'll get a job done. I cannot be waiting, not with my clients. They need to be thinking ahead, predicting the next move and outcome, and making the necessary plans to navigate whatever the landscape ahead dictates.

CHAPTER 8

THE $30,000 DINNER

Interview with ... Deepak Ohri
CEO, LEBUA HOTELS AND RESORTS

I f you have ever eaten at a rooftop bar or restaurant you can thank Deepak Ohri. While he did not invent the concept of al fresco atop a skyscraper, his astute promotions of The Dome at lebua certainly popularized the concept that is now nearly de rigeur in the high-end food and beverage scene. And while much of the revenue is from aspirational consumers, getting a high profile crowd is important. More importantly, getting the Super Rich to fork over lots of dough for the privilege takes great finesse. Ohri showed his skills by conceptualizing the Million Baht Dinner, then successfully selling it to UHNWs featuring six courses, each cooked by a different Michelin star chef.

Were you nervous about selling such a high priced dinner?

For me, it's very difficult to sell something that is a hundred bucks, in my career. When it comes to selling something that's $10,000, $20,000, it's very easy.

When you did the dinner, how many people ended up buying it?

Forty people, twenty-one were paid.

Did you meet all of the twenty-one who bought the dinner?

I had met them all personally to sell them this dinner.

What type of interaction was there to get them to actually buy it?

It was very easy to sell, not because I was doing it, but because it was such an experience. I'll tell you the logic. We were giving them something that they could never have gotten in their entire life. These people are billionaires. And that's what they look for, things which are very difficult to come by.

We gave them food cooked by six different Michelin star chefs at one place, course by course. We gave them wine from different regions, glass by glass. Ninety-nine percent of high-end restaurants wouldn't sell these wines by the glass. And they were drinking them glass-by-glass without the guilt that they'd have a bottle and have to waste it.

It was an experience that was an easy sell actually. You go to these people and talk to them about the experience, and never talk to them about the price. They never asked me about the price. But at the end they said, 'ok, so how should we pay?' I said, we'll charge your card, and we got the card number, but they never asked us about the price. They were so thrilled about the experience that they never even complained about the price.

Where did the people come from?

They were from different continents. Most from Asia, but some from Italy, some Europeans, some Americans.

Did they come specifically for the dinner?

Many flew in on private jets, because some of the international people didn't want to be at the airport because they'd be photographed.

Since you met them, were they known people or were they basically unknown wealthy people?

No, they're not very known people. Once you become known, it's hard to sell people something, because they expect everything to be given on a platter for free because you're promoting it.

Do you know how these people made their money?

They're in casinos, shipping, oil. A mix of businesses.

Did you have to do anything differently in terms of the way you worked with them versus the typical guests?

All of these guests were about enjoying their life and experiences. How they pay, maybe by credit card or whatever, I don't know, but they really know how to enjoy their lives. And for these people, these things really matter. They get very picky about their experiences. I can relate to them in terms of eating well, living well, even though I'm not very rich. They're very principled people, they're very ethical people, and they're very logical people. They expect principles; they respect the stand you've taken.

They get finicky about dirty tablecloths, when the waiter is taking too much time at each the table and when their wine glass is empty. They'll get very upset if you try to give them an explanation of why something isn't working. Just make it right.

Was most of the dialogue directly with the person, through 'gatekeepers' or with personal assistants?

It was all direct dealing. It took me nine months to get the people. I must have met 375 people.

How did you identify the people you wanted to talk to about the dinner?

I read magazines. I read interviews. I go to them. The people I didn't get was where I was dealing with their personal assistant or gate-keeper.

So you did your own prospecting on wealthy people?

Yes, and I also worked with a lady who's into a lot of things. She was the first customer. I met her in Hong Kong.

Did any come as referrals from other customers?

There were a few that came with friends. One guest came with three other guests. He didn't even drink wine—and someone asked him why are you spending so much money if you don't drink? He said, 'I've stopped drinking, food is life and I cannot get this food any-where else.'

Did you do the Million Baht Dinner again since, or was this the only time?

We got a lot of press about the Million Baht Dinner, and now we're plan-ning on doing something different—a million-dollar dinner!

We'll do it once the business comes back. In the next eighteen months. It'll only be for ten guests.

From the time you talk to somebody about the Million Baht Dinner, how long did it take someone to say yes?

It took months. In the business of luxury, unknown people are your best customers.

Did these customers fit any type of profile, in terms of style?

We had customers yesterday (at The Dome) buying, for $30,000, champagne and caviar, and they were very simply dressed. Wearing Nike sneakers, jeans, and a t-shirt. They were visitors.

Is it common for people to drop money like that?

We used to have a very regular customer. I once spoke about how there were some Thai guests who spend an incredible amount of money. He got upset that I spoke about this. I play golf with him these days, but when he comes to the restaurant he doesn't want me to talk to him or recognize him. The rule of thumb in luxury is that anyone asking for attention is not spending the most money. The people spending the most money want the least publicity. It's about the experience and the product. They don't need that attention. I don't need attention when things go right.

Our best local spender came to us and we just gave him a table. My manager opened a bottle of Romani Conti. He said, go for it. It was 5.8 million baht—$60,000. He was very happy. He went to another place and they asked for his membership card and he got very upset. These rich people need emotional contact. If you connect with them emotionally, they'll stay with you forever.

Do you think people are afraid to connect with them emotionally because they're in awe of these people?

We're doing something called 'Experience of Epicurean' for next year, where we're going to have thirty people stay at the hotel, and walk them through the various wine and food, meet the staff, have food cooked right in front of them. I don't meet them. I'll meet them at some point, but not at the hotel. They don't want me to meet them at the hotel. The day I start meeting them is the day I kill my own business. They want to meet the waiter, the cook, but we can't overdo it.

SUMMARY

Young tech billionaires want to stay at grand dame hotels with their families, while newly divorced fifty-something global CEOs are looking for party suites at trendy boutique hotels for the getaway with their new girlfriend. Pets can influence purchasing decisions. Hundreds of thousands of dollars can be spent shuttling pets between divorced parents on private jets. Wives will choose the airplane based on the size of the bathroom, but often husbands decide where to go on vacation.

Personal Shoppers for the Super Rich can be like a psychologist, often making house calls to the Super Rich's homes and private jets. Sales can run easily into the tens of thousands of dollars per visit. It is not unusual for a head of state to keep another world leader waiting while choosing patterns for his shirts.

For everyone selling to the Super Rich, confidentiality is key. And, listening is critical. In rare instances, the sales superstars of luxury become family friends, but nearly always it's a business relationship based on high levels of service and trust. The superstars are expected to be accessible 24/7, yet their busy Super Rich clients are often hard to reach directly, protected by their gatekeepers and personal assistants who can muddle the communications.

The Super Rich often have ideas of what they want, but also are seeking recommendations and validation of their ideas. Contrary to perceptions, the Super Rich are influenced by advertising, public relations and media just like the rest of us. A popular child's game can inspire a six figure themed trip built around Pokémon. The Super Rich often have little in-depth knowledge about the brand heritage and product lines of what they are buying. Some don't care. And, information overload on product specifications can kill a sale.

While most of the Super Rich are pleasant to relate to and are low key, some can be demanding, and some sales superstars of luxury don't think they are worth the trouble. The superstars have no problem 'firing' Super Rich clients.

The tastes of the Super Rich are much more diverse than is generally assumed. While you can find the Super Rich playing polo (after all, you have to be rich to own a team and fly your horses around) or at Art Basel Miami (where several hundred private jets land), you can find just as many, if not more, attending Formula 1 racing, or in luxury boxes at professional football games on Sundays. While the Super Rich sit on the boards of opera houses and museums, and are large supporters of the arts, you can equally find them big wave surfing off the coast of Costa Rica, hunting in the West, fishing in New Zealand, kite-surfing off Puerto Rico, or extreme skiing in Iceland. Hundreds of private jets owned by the Super Rich descend on places such as Baton Rouge, South Bend, Austin and Norman for college football games, attending alumni-hosted parties in tents with chandeliers and celebrity chefs.

While luxury companies have rightly identified philanthropy as important to customers, and often make it a pillar of their marketing strategies, the Super Rich already have their own charities and causes they care about. In other words—if you want to buy favor with a Super Rich client, support their cause. A brand's support of its corporately chosen charities is unlikely to resonate.

Most of all, if you are looking to grow your business with the Super Rich, you need to cast your net beyond Wall Street, Hollywood and Palm Beach. Between the coasts, farmers in Ohio, auto parts manufacturers in Kentucky, car dealers in Minnesota and ranchers in Texas, are some of the biggest spenders on watches, jewelry and fashion, yet do not fit the stereotype of what a high-spending luxury customer is supposed to look like. Newly minted tech titans in the West are traveling the world on their private jets, and in less than a decade, have transitioned from sleeping on couches to lounging on Frette linens as they gain comfort spending their newly earned fortunes. Sellers to the Super Rich don't let stereotypes get in the way—they close six figure jewelry and watch sales on the back of a pick-up truck at a cattle ranch, at an alligator farm in Louisiana, as well as at Park Avenue and Beverly Hills mansions.

Price is rarely a critical factor. The perception of the rich getting rich by haggling for a better deal did not strike true with the sales superstars of luxury.

For luxury marketers, a smart UHNW strategy is more important than ever. A strategy that addresses and relates to the special access needs and extraordinary behaviors of the Super Rich is key in supporting the sellers on the front line.

While each of the sales superstars of luxury interviewed has a different approach, a commonality is not to make assumptions about what Super Rich like and don't like. They listen, take notes and keep records so they don't have to ask twice, they assist in non-related endeavors when asked, and respect the type of communications their Super Rich clients prefer. These customers require service providers who can consistently execute above & beyond, who can make the transaction process simple and confidential, and who can serve with the utmost trust.

ABOUT THE AUTHORS

Doug Gollan

With a background as a journalist, Doug Gollan made the transition early in his career into magazine ad sales, and then into management working his way up the ladder to Group Publisher of trade weekly Travel Agent Magazine, and then to Group President of Elite Traveler Media Group. Over 30 years he has been responsible for sales teams selling B2C and B2B media solutions to companies across travel, luxury, automotive, spirits, fashion and financial services from American Airlines and American Express to Cartier, British Airways, Chanel, Four Seasons, Gucci, Hertz Rent-a-Car, Hilton Hotels, Mercedes-Benz, Patron, Ralph Lauren, VISA Worldwide and more.

During Doug's tenure in the 1990's Travel Agent Magazine rose from seventh place in its category to one of the top five magazines in the US ranked by Advertising Age, based on ad pages.

In 2001, Doug co-founded Elite Traveler, the first and only magazine distributed worldwide aboard private jets that has had its circulation successfully audited, creating the most affluent audience of any print media in the world. At its peak, the magazine generated over $15 million in ad revenue.

Since leaving Elite Traveler in 2014, he has launched *DG Amazing Experiences*, a weekly "CEO-style" e-newsletter focused on travel and lifestyle that is receiving critical acclaim. He also serves on the Management Board of Travel Market Report, a leading B2B website and daily newsletter for top travel agents. Additionally, he works as a consultant to companies seeking to build their position with UHNW consumers.

Doug published *23 Ways to Create More Sales Opportunities in 25 Minutes* (2014), a book that taps his 25 years' worth of sales and revenue expertise. He is considered an expert on Ultra High Net Worth consumers and has been quoted in The Wall Street Journal, The New York Times, Forbes.com as well as appearing on NBC Nightly News, Fox Business News and The Travel Channel. Doug was co-author of *The Sky's the Limit:*

Marketing Luxury to the New Jet Set (2007) and a contributor to *Taking the Reins: Insights Into the World of Ultra-Wealthy Inheritors* (2014). Doug also publishes a popular blog on marketing to "the 1 percent" at doug-gollan.com.

Michael Calman

A strategic innovation specialist and marketer of iconic luxury lifestyle brands, Michael Calman has decades of experience in retail marketing and creating exceptional customer engagement. He has extensive background in omni-channel marketing, merchandising and revenue integration across specialty stores, e-commerce, wholesale and catalogs. His C-level marketing spans the luxury spectrum, from aspirational through Ultra High Net Worth customers, and from accessible luxury-priced handbags to private jets.

Prior to founding Calman Consulting, LLC in 2006, Michael's experience was built on marketing creative powerhouse brands. His corporate marketing leadership background includes Calvin Klein, Coach and Bergdorf Goodman, where ground-breaking initiatives and strategic partnerships were developed and implemented—achieving preeminent brand recognition, CRM productivity and market share. During his tenure at Calvin Klein, as Founder and Managing Director of CRK Advertising, Michael was the executive producer of several transformative marketing initiatives, including the highly acclaimed Calvin Klein Jeans and 'Obsession' fragrance television, print and outdoor campaigns. As VP of Marketing at Coach, he repositioned the company from a handbag merchandise concentration to an accessories brand by leading the product development of accessory collections. At Bergdorf Goodman, the world's leading luxury goods department store, as SVP of Marketing, Michael steered the development of BergdorfGoodman. com, was the founder and publisher of Bergdorf Goodman Magazine, and architected a strategic alliance based customer loyalty program. As Chief Marketing Officer of CitationShares, he directed the Vector JetCard launch, establishing the card as the industry's most accessible entry to private jet travel.

Calman Consulting, LLC, provides business insight, turnaround strategies, omni-platform marketing and digital programs for legacy brands and innovative start-ups, focused on luxury, fashion, specialty retail and real estate companies, and communications agencies.

Michael has Master of Business Administration and Bachelor of Arts degrees from New York University, and conducts speaking engagements to corporations, trade groups and academic institutions. He is also an avid racing sailor, including competing as a finalist in the United States Olympic Sailing Trials.

Daniel Wade

A 30-year veteran in travel, Daniel Wade is an expert in partnership marketing and luxury lifestyle media with significant experience in consumer & B2B media, brand positioning and sales development with global leaders in travel/hospitality, yachting, private jet and the luxury goods sectors. He is currently SVP & Co-Publisher of TravelMarketReport.com, a leading B2B information provider to North American travel agents, and is directing sales, marketing and partnership development for the website. Daniel is also a consultant for luxury businesses and is Head of Strategic Partnerships for yachting industry leader Northrop & Johnson.

In 2001, he co-founded Elite Traveler with Doug Gollan. As President and Publisher, Daniel built Elite Traveler's multi-media platforms, including Elitetraveler.com and Elite Traveler TV, and attracted a blue-chip list of marketing partners. Prior to starting Elite Traveler, he was Executive Associate Publisher of Travel Agent Magazine responsible for worldwide sales, and leading the publication to top 10 rankings by Advertising Age, by ad pages run. He also developed and sold integrated travel agent training and educational programs, and helped create Travel Agent University, the first online training portal for travel retailers. Daniel was also on the "bleeding-edge" of one of the most disruptive periods in the travel industry as a pioneer in the online travel arena with Preview Travel (Travelocity) and before that, served in senior positions with Certified Vacations and Delta Air Lines.

A specialist in sales and marketing to Ultra High Net Worth consumers, Daniel has been a speaker at global tourism, real estate development, private aviation and mega-yacht industry conferences. A native of the United Kingdom, Daniel now resides in South Florida.

Made in the USA
Lexington, KY
28 November 2016